Royalty on Horseback

Judith Campbell

Royalty on Horseback

Doubleday & Company, Inc

Garden City, New York

Previous pages, left to right:
Edward VIII as Prince of
Wales at Hawthorn Hill in
1923; Queen Elizabeth II as a
small girl on one of her
favourite ponies; King George
VI at the Trooping the Colour
on 12 June 1947, when he was
accompanied by Princess
Elizabeth (below left); King
George V (centre) at a review
of Horse Guards and Life
Guards in 1927; Queen Victoria
with her ghillie, John Brown,
1863

Designed by Paul Watkins and Florianne Henfield

Picture research by Anne-Marie Ehrlich

First published in Great Britain in 1974
Copyright © 1974 by Judith Campbell
and Sidgwick and Jackson Limited

ISBN 0 385 08851 5

Library of Congress Catalog Card Number 74-17703

Printed in Great Britain

1 From Normans to Tudors
Many horses are requisites for kings...and queens

Above: The Great Seal of the Realm graces documents of the highest importance. The obverse side always shows the Monarch mounted and depicts the prestige of the royal chargers, the significant link between horses and the throne

Previous pages: Each year on that Saturday in early June chosen to celebrate her Official Birthday, Queen Elizabeth II rides from Buckingham Palace to Horseguard's Parade to take the salute at the Trooping the Colour

On the obverse side of the Great Seals of the Realm belonging to the reigns of Queen Elizabeth I and Queen Elizabeth II of England, the sovereigns are, as always, depicted on horseback. Both are seated side-saddle, each according to the mode of her time, with one queen mounted on a high-stepping, richly caparisoned Courser of State, the other riding a quality animal of the kind used for the ceremony of Trooping the Colour.

It was natural that for centuries one side of the stylized Great Seals should depict the reigning monarch on a horse. A handsome courser was one of the emblems of the power and prestige of the crown, during all those eras when horses were as essential to the throne as they were to everyday life. In those times, if not today, it would have been unthinkable to omit the sovereign's mount from the token of supreme authority.

In the Middle East and in parts of Europe and Asia the strong link between monarchy and horses was conspicuous thousands of years before the birth of Christ. In England it became apparent much later, chiefly because until about the eleventh century the majority of English horses were of the small Celtic pony type, very different from the oriental animals of the east—and 'however handsome a man may be, he appears insignificant on a little horse. . . .' Then the Saxons, like the Scandinavians who were their enemies,

continued to fight solely on foot long after this was outmoded on the Continent.

Alfred the Great was the first English king to appoint a royal horsemaster, and his recorded precedent of royal interest was furthered during the reign of Athelstane. Athelstane esteemed horses sufficiently to fix a scale of compensation for injuries to a borrowed horse, and after a gift of 'running horses' from the King of France forbade their export from his dominions except as royal gifts. William the Conqueror and the House of Normandy brought larger horses, Normandy chargers used as 'cavalry', and Spanish stallions, plus a tradition of horsemanship as a dimension of the great social and cultural changes of the Norman Conquest.

To William I and William II, to Henry I and Stephen, horses represented the might of the crown. They were as indispensable as the huge circular mounds which were topped with a fortress and possessed of an outer court from which the king's armoured horsemen rode out to enforce the new feudal order of the land.

The kings of the earlier Middle Ages and their knights rode so-called Great Horses to war, but as men were not then as big as they are today and the weighty plate-armour was not yet invented, their war-horses and the prized destriers, kept exclusively for jousting, were more of the stamp of twentieth-century cavalry

En route for Rouen, Harold had a foretaste of the type of Norman horse that was soon to play an important role in the Norman Conquest

horses than the imagined huge animals of Shire-horse dimensions. But although these chargers were faster and more handy than many visualize, and considerably more so than the lumbering Great Horses of Tudor times, the Crusaders found them no match for the speedy, quick-turning Arabs which their adversaries, the infidel, bestrode. They therefore wasted no time in re-horsing themselves with animals of some oriental breeding, stallions which, as always, were carefully and specially trained for warfare.

Richard Coeur de Lion, the most famous of the knights errant and a leader of the Third Crusade, was a skilled horseman: a fact he demonstrated at the Cyprus landing by dashing ashore and, with the aid of his lance, vaulting—armour and all—on to the back of a 'common' horse, in order to gallop after the caitiff Emperor Isaak and challenge him to combat. He had two favourite war-horses in the Holy Land, a Cypriot of Arab strain and a Turcoman, both relatively light and fast and fully capable of exploits such as the incident when one, bearing the king, had to leap clean over a charging wild boar.

While King Richard was absent from England, first engaging Saladin's champions in combat and then languishing in an Austrian prison, his treacherous brother John was busying himself with annexing the crown. After that came such far-reaching if mundane matters of policy as importing a number of heavy stallions from north Germany and the Low Countries; transactions which were to increase the size and type of a section of the English horse population, but which were scarcely productive of hot-blooded animals such as Favell and Lyard, imported by King Richard on his return. These were 'running' horses, 'swifter than dromedaries' and considered beyond price by their royal owner.

Grading horses for use, partly by size, was first practised in the Middle Ages. The largest were kept for carrying the knights, and in every reign the royal horsemaster was on the look-out for well-trained, impressive stallions, capable of enhancing the prestige of the king in the eyes of his subjects. Yet during the Hundred Years War Edward III, who expended vast sums on his great cavalry department, chose to review his army, before the vital battle of Crécy, from the back of a small and gentle white palfrey. On this unimposing animal the king rode up and down amongst the ranks of his troops, encouraging them and entreating them to 'guard his honour and defend his right', with 'sweetness' and a 'cheerful countenance', and to such good effect that the English immediately defeated the French in a notable victory.

King Richard II is said to have loved his Roan Barbary—a 'foreigner' most likely to have been Arabian or Barb—like a son. But if he ever used the words put by Shakespeare into the mouth of his descendant, Richard III, and even rhetorically offered his 'kingdom for a horse', he would more probably have had in mind the powerful black stallion on which, clad in chain-mail and bearing a formidable battle axe, he led his men-at-arms to war. For to the monarchs of these centuries their chargers were still as essential, if not quite as highly trained, as the destriers they trusted to bear them victoriously in the joust, a sport not yet relegated from being the noblest of all the knightly arts of combat.

Then, during the fifteenth century, the long-bow, the deadliest weapon as yet devised, and first claimed as the English national weapon at Crécy and Poitiers, destroyed the supremacy of the armoured knight in battle. Even in the reign of Henry II Welsh guerillas had been known to pin an armoured knight's thigh to his horse with an arrow from a long-bow. Chain-mail was no protection against an arrow-hail of clothyard shafts, and the razor-sharp points could also find chinks even in the new armour-plate. The answer seemed to be to pile more and heavier armour on the knight, and complete bards of plate-armour on his already burdened horse.

As a young man, Henry VIII imported an Italian armourer to employ his skills in fashioning a complete plate-armour for him and his horse, the entire surface to be decorated with engraving and covered in silver-gilt. The handsome young king must then have presented a most splendid spectacle, but now that the lighter chain-mail was outmoded, already he and his knights needed a sturdier type of charger. As the years added their burden of flesh, King Harry found himself ever more dependent on horses like those descendants of the heavy beasts imported three centuries before by King John.

By this time the total weight of even a less exalted, and less obese, knight-at-arms, together with his bulky saddle, hefty weapons, and horse's extensive furnishing, added up to around thirty-two stone, and of necessity his mount had to be a massive creature, more ponderous than fleet of foot. So the king imported ever more Great Horses from Flanders and ordered the reduction or elimination of all small stallions—policies which resulted in his 'cavalry' becoming more or less invulnerable to bow-men, but so slow that they were of small effect; a fact that mattered little since the newest weapon of war was gunpowder, and no plate-armour, however thick, would stop a musket-ball. The Great Horse of Tudor times was therefore gradually delegated from the battlefield to the tilt yard, and eventually to agriculture.

Tilting and the tournaments, which were originally effective battle-training, and where the joust was as often *à l'outrance* (to the death) as *à plaisance* (for fun), now became innocuous, magnificent

Opposite above: Jousting, that favoured sport of medieval monarchs and their knights, was included in the celebrations ordered by Henry VIII to honour his Queen, Katherine of Aragon, and to celebrate the birth of their son, Henry, Duke of Cornwall

Below: With his own increasing bulk and the weight of armour with which he and his chargers were furnished, it is small wonder that Henry VIII favoured 'great horses'

and highly popular spectator sports. The carousal, an off-shoot that was a kind of elaborate mounted pageant (which survives today in the 'parade' in American Western horse shows), was very fashionable with the court and nobility. But if the heavy courser's day as a fighting unit was ending, his specialized training—those elegant high-school 'airs' such as the levade and breath-taking capriole, all spectacular if of questionable practical fighting use—were not. Such schooling, and horsemanship in general, began to be developed as a science. And although King Henry VII, in many ways a shrewd monarch but no great horseman, had ordered his mount for state occasions to be starved into tractability, his son, Henry VIII, already an excellent rider, took to the new sport with enthusiasm. He introduced a skilled riding-master to Hampton Court and concentrated, with his usual one hundred per cent zest for some new diversion, on the principles of the manege.

Many of the training methods imbibed by King Henry make strange reading today. Even he found that if the procedure of introducing a live hedgehog under the tail of one of his older horses that had turned 'nappy' undoubtedly induced his animal to move forward as required, it also presented a new problem in the horse's reluctance thereafter to stop. Yet a book written by an Italian master of equitation eight years before King Henry's daughter, Elizabeth, began her reign (a book that soon spread its principles of training throughout western Europe), contains many of the basic elements of horsemanship and equine understanding. It also promoted a new interest in riding and horses, and an awareness of them beyond their purely functional role in Elizabethan life.

As Hugh Latimer, the English bishop who ended his days at the stake in 1555, once remarked: 'Many horses are requisite for a king', and the truism applies also to a queen.

Queen Elizabeth bred horses for war, some of which by then carried troops armed with arquebuses, at the royal Tutbury and Malmesbury studs. They were upstanding animals, which trotted as opposed to ambled, one of the requisites laid down by her father in the laws concerning the breeding of remounts. She kept 'Barbaries' at Hampton Court, oriental animals noted for their easy 'travelynge pace'—a tripple that was neither quite trot nor amble—and they were used also for breeding 'swift runners'. There too were finely made and speedy Spanish Jennets, of the same gait and considered very suitable mounts for medieval ladies, the mares much in demand for breeding palfreys—those small but noble-looking animals whose gentle disposition made them the most favoured of all riding nags.

It was 'ambling palfreys' which, just before her accession, conveyed the Princess Elizabeth and that part of her retinue composed of twelve ladies—all somewhat impracticably clad in white

KING HENRY VIII.
ARMOUR FOR FIELD AND TILT
1535-40
HORSE ARMOUR
c.1530

satin—from Hatfield House to Enfield Close in order to hunt the hart.

Like her father, the queen was an assiduous follower of the chase and was still hunting the red and fallow deer through the royal forests when she was well into her sixties. But despite the sensible length of her riding skirt, designed by herself just to cover the stirrup, and her possible use of the safer side-saddle pommel invented by her contemporary, Catherine de' Medici, it is unlikely that any great speed was involved in the sport, and certainly there would have been no jumping. A charter of Henry I had helped amend the ferocious Norman 'Forest Law', by entitling the citizens of London to hunt deer freely in the Chiltern Hundreds, Surrey and Middlesex—with the added privilege in that latter county of being able to hunt the wolf 'up to the northern gate of the city'. Partly owing to this, and with the needs of population encroaching on the forest country, the woodland denizen, the deer, had started to become less common three hundred years before Elizabeth came to the throne. And the version of venerie the queen sometimes employed, when she shot driven deer with her arbalist (cross-bow), must have further decimated the herds and certainly did away with any need for a fast hunting horse. Whether the queen was out hawking with her nobles, or whether she was deer-hunting, her mount was a palfrey rather than the more spirited and powerful animals used by gentlemen for the chase.

The queen chose a white palfrey, small in stature and sober by nature, that was loaned by the Cecils, as a rostrum for delivering her rousing exhortation, at Tilbury, to her subjects of 'loyal heart and goodwill' threatened by an imminent Spanish invasion. She came amongst them 'scrawny, painted, bewigged and the wrong side of fifty', yet still generating the magic quality of leadership and inspiring them with her heroic words. There was of course an official painting, from which numerous engravings were taken, to record the historic event, but in this the queen's horse is depicted as a large and splendid war-horse or Courser of State, the type of animal in the artist's opinion more suited to its royal rider on such a memorable occasion. Only· in the small, stylized picture of the queen and her horse on that day, to be seen in a Norfolk church, is her mount shown to be the palfrey it undoubtedly was. There was a subsequent portrait of the animal itself, inevitably re-christened Tilbury and much cherished by the Cecils, but even in this, although the type is plain, everything that might be measured against the horse to demonstrate its true lack of stature has been carefully excluded.

On the evening before her crowning Queen Elizabeth had come in procession seated in a litter, or open chariot, not unlike a

mobile Elizabethan four-poster bed, which was borne by two horses, one in front and one at the back, and with a knight attendant at each corner to support the canopy. Directly behind rode the master of the horse, the then young and handsome Robert Dudley, leading the queen's Palfrey of State—a substitute for the Courser of State, too spirited a type to carry a side-saddle, which would have been there had the monarch been a king. And this was an important unit in the vast procession, chiefly composed of a glittering cavalcade of horsemen, which took many hours to progress from the Tower of London to Westminster Palace.

By Tudor times the system of transport, and the economy, were sufficiently advanced to sustain all the ramifications of the court in one city, and in London it no longer lacked a resting place large enough to contain it throughout the year. It was no longer necessary for the sovereign and his establishment to move around the country to collect, that is eat, the royal dues rendered in kind, for all but the few weeks of crown-wearings at Westminster and Winchester and Gloucester. But Queen Elizabeth still took her retinue to make some annual progresses around her realm, no doubt to some extent to strengthen and test the loyalty of her subjects. Sometimes she stayed at one of the great houses of the nobility: visits which enhanced the prestige but depleted the pocket of the host, and threw each selected ménage into a fine state of confusion and trepidation weeks before the royal arrival. Sometimes she elected to take up residence at one of the royal palaces retained

Queen Elizabeth I progresses to Nonsuch using one of the 'luxurious' first coaches – a mode of transport she secretly despised

in different parts of the country. But wherever the queen and her court went there was need of a great train of horses, of all shapes and sizes and different uses, to convey there and back the royal retinue and their baggage.

On these progresses the queen might at times elect to ride pillion behind one of her male courtiers, just as on one occasion she rode to St Paul's Cathedral behind her master of the horse. Or she might choose to go at least part of the way by coach, the form of transport first seen on English roads in 1555, an envied 'luxury' enjoyed only by the wealthy nobility. For although the queen disliked this form of transport, considering it effeminate, and found her original coach built by William Rippon in 1564 far from comfortable, she did replace it with a Dutch model that proved more to her taste.

Not that any coach of the period, for all its costly trappings inside, could have been much more than bearable as, springless until the eighteenth century and as yet lacking the ease eventually brought by suspending the body with leather braces, it lumbered and bounced from rut to rut along the rough tracks that served as roads. And since it took strong horses to pull the royal or any other coach, suitable teams had to be included along with the riding animals—the Jennets and ambling palfreys for the queen and her ladies, and the nags and hobbies, with amblers and 'gentil hors' (imported coursers) for hunting, for the nobles and gentlemen of the court. There were rouncies and cobs for the pages and servants, Great Horses for the troops and gentlemen-at-arms, and a huge array of pack animals: ponies and donkeys which on departure after a stay at one of the royal palaces had to convey, in addition to the vast amount of baggage deemed indispensable for all such journeyings, every smallest piece of furniture and every stitch of hangings, so that only the bare walls remained.

But the years passed, all forty-four of that progressive and magnificent reign, until even that indomitable character, Queen Elizabeth I, could no longer make her journeyings; came the time when, however willing the spirit, the old limbs were too stiff to ride or hunt or go hawking. But even at the end, when a lesser soul would have accepted defeat and taken to her bed, Elizabeth of England still sat stiff-backed in her chair, defying the death that claimed her eventually in the small hours of 25 March 1603.

And that moment was the signal for a messenger, awaiting the call for weeks, to mount the first of a relay of horses ready saddled; to mount and ride nearly four hundred miles in sixty-six hours to Scotland and Holyrood House, to acclaim James Stuart, James VI of Scotland, England's new King James I, the first of the House of Stuart.

Opposite: Like her father, Queen Bess loved the chase in all its forms (above left and right). But the medieval side-saddle offered small security and, however skilled her horsemanship, however intrepid her heart, there was not much speed involved in the Queen's hunting. Queen Elizabeth did not aspire to riding a splendid courser of the type often imported for her gentlemen's pleasure, her mount was usually that small animal of gentle disposition called a palfrey. Even at Tilbury (below) on the historic occasion when the ageing Queen's fiery rhetoric roused her army to await with eagerness the expected assault of the Armada from Spain, her chosen rostrum was on the back of a sober little palfrey

2 The Stuarts
Establishing the sport of kings

At James I's coronation service, for the first time English was used instead of the customary Latin, but the innovation could be said to have been offset at the coronation banquet by the medieval presence of the King's Champion. This was a fully armed knight, reining his horse to issue challenges on the monarch's behalf, an outmoded custom dating from the coronation of Richard II, and in this case as inappropriate as it was chivalrous and picturesque.

For this was a king who had the estimable ambition to be a peace-maker. He believed the pen to be mightier than the sword, even if he lacked the perception to realize that his style of appeasement too often stirred up the trouble it sought to avoid. Part of his pacifism was also due to the fact that a drawn sword, or any naked steel, made him feel physically ill. For this reason he avoided whenever possible any ceremonies, such as reviewing his troops, and it is unlikely that in his reign the royal studs contained any war-horses for the monarch's personal use, particularly as the mere sight of a Great Horse is said to have 'bored him to tears'. James I has gone down in history as the last king to ride a palfrey for a public event. From then onwards, until after the death of William III, the sovereign always appeared to his subjects, on ceremonial occasions, mounted on a Neapolitan Courser of State, one of those impressive animals derived from Spanish Andalusians which were already being imported in King James's reign but which James himself would not contemplate riding on account of their military connection.

None of this infers that James I was not a good horseman, or that he was disinterested in horses, even if on one occasion his mount did manage to throw its royal rider head-first through the ice covering the New River. But the king had just come from attending a convivial dinner and took the episode in such good part that after being rescued by an attendant, and duly horror-struck noblemen, who pulled him out by his royal boots, the monarch merely laughed at the misadventure and rode merrily off to bed.

King James enjoyed hawking, and had such a passion for hunting that he wrote a long treatise in praise of both the 'noble sport' and of games on horseback—diversions such as the 'wild-goose chase' which entailed galloping cross-country over obstacles, with betting on the results to liven it up. The king also made sure that the royal princes were taught to hunt 'with running hounds'—as opposed to shooting with guns or bows or using greyhounds.

It is recorded that in the first year of his reign James granted a pardon to a Sir Pexall Brocas, 'for all riots and unlawful assemblies before 20 March last past'. This was a knight of Gascon origin who was one of the last to lay claim to the hereditary title of master or keeper of the Royal Buckhounds. This was an office which usually combined the charge of the royal studs with that of the royal

Opposite: King Charles I's elegance of person was well-matched by his graceful horsemanship

hunting establishment—and invoked a precedent that goes back at least as far as the fourteenth century, when some of the de Brocas family settled in England. By Henry VIII's reign the constitution of the establishment had become unsuitable to requirements. That sovereign therefore started a Privy Pack, its masters holding office at the king's pleasure (one of the first being Lord Rochford, Anne Boleyn's brother). As would be expected, the Privy Buckhounds were strenuously opposed by the hereditary masters. But although the new office was revoked by Queen Mary, the Privy Pack was re-established under Queen Elizabeth and her successor, and in the early seventeenth century the hereditary office became obsolete.

Apparently King James did not indulge in the scientific equitation of the manege—the *haute école* that was to prove as attractive to his son, Charles, as it had been to Henry VIII—presumably again because of its military association. But during this reign racing, the subsequent 'sport of kings', began to be organized and, quickly gaining in popularity, together with games and dancing won the seal of royal approval. And that despite the diatribes of an anti-racing fanatic who considered the sport, and the extensive betting which was an integral part, the source of 'profanity, cursing, brawling, quarrelling, bad example and idleness'.

To King James, when Duke of York, must go too the honour of having 'discovered' Newmarket, originally as an excellent hare-hunting centre after he had killed six of his quarry with his own hounds near a place called Buckland. Later, both he and his brother organized races there, and in another way he influenced the future of the sport. For although the progeny of the oriental horses, imported for the Royal Tutbury Stud during King James's reign, were sold and dispersed in 1651, they set the precedent for a type that was to play no small part in the evolution of the supreme racing machine of all time, the English Thoroughbred.

King Charles I—inadvisedly clad in white, 'the ancient colour for a victim', instead of the usual purple—decided to come by water from Whitehall to Westminster instead of on horseback. But he was a good horseman, accomplished in the art of the manege, and during the Stuart epoch—apart from their necessity for everyday existence—horses increased in importance as a source of pleasure. During this period elegant horsemanship became a top requisite of the royal and nobly born, and with this development came the need for the more refined and hot-blooded breeds which could demonstrate the skills of a good rider, and which continued to oust the powerful armour-carriers still primarily considered suitable for war. When the king and his French Catholic queen, Henrietta Maria, went riding together, they were likely to be mounted on a couple of those 'over-valued pigmy baubles', by now widely bred instead of the traditional war-horses, and considered by the reactionary only suitable for such fripperies as racing and hunting.

Early in his reign King Charles was presented with a petition warning him of the shortage of Great Horses—not two thousand could be procured if required at short notice—with the consequent fear that the supremacy of the British cavalry in war was being affected, and that 'the French horses were in every way superior to ours'. But the king paid little heed to the warning; and when in fact war came it was not in the familiar form of battles with the French or other traditional enemies on the Continent, but in the fearful form of civil war.

Because of King James's run-down of the armed forces, neither the king's followers nor the parliamentarians started with a trained force, but although, apart from this basic equality, the Cavaliers were in many other ways at a disadvantage, their horses and men were, given the right leader, of the type to be more easily and quickly welded into cavalry than those of their adversaries. In the king's nephew, a dashing young man of twenty-two, they found just the leadership required. And under Prince Rupert those hard-riding squires and their grooms, together with the nobles who were automatically 'for the king', were mostly mounted, not on slow and obsolete Great Horses, but on the handy, medium-weight animals they used for hunting, with the dragoons riding 'good squat cobs'. These animals could produce the speed that was better protection against musketry than any heavy armour, and had the physical ability to charge at the gallop and disrupt the musketeers while they were re-loading.

In very rough or enclosed ground the infantryman, more often than not a pikeman, could be better value than the horseman, but in the open landscape of much of the country of those days the cavalry proved superior and won most of the decisive battles of the war.

By 1644 the initial tide of success had passed from the royalist party to Parliament's forces. The 'Roundheads' were then commanded by Oliver Cromwell, who had been at Edgehill (the first battle of the war and a royalist victory), and noted Prince Rupert's spirited tactics and the superiority of his horses. Cromwell had then wasted no time in raising and training his force of 'Ironsides', the well-disciplined, well-mounted troops drawn from the yeoman and freeholding classes. These troops shattered Prince Rupert's army at Marston Moor that year, and, after delivering a further crushing defeat to the king and his cause at Naseby a year later, they secured the final royalist defeat at Torrington in 1646.

The sequence of events which brought King Charles I to the block now moved to their tragic conclusion, and in 1653 Oliver Cromwell became Lord Protector.

The saga of the exiled rakish Prince Charles, who was born on 29 May 1630, and who, as Charles II, succeeded to the throne without a kingdom in 1649, brought further bloody fighting to the English countryside. But after the death of Cromwell, and just when the royalist cause seemed at lowest ebb, the apparently secure Protectorate began to fall apart. Englishmen, tired of a parliament and army now continually at odds, turned their thoughts longingly towards a king once more, and in 1660 the eldest son of Charles I was restored to the throne.

One of the first royal orders issued when 'the king enjoyed his own again', was that Cromwell's horses, including the seven that were 'said to be the best in England', be straight way taken to the Royal Mews for the 'service of His Majesty'. They were good horses too, for although the Protector, a fine rider and at heart an enthusiastic sportsman, had had to humour the fanatics with a temporary ban on racing, bull-baiting, cock-fighting, hunting, hawking and (oddly) football, he continued to import a supply of eastern horses, from Mediterranean agents instructed to procure the very best available.

Even as a boy, Charles II's horsemanship had excited the admiration of the Duke of Newcastle, his eminent tutor in the art. And, as King, his accomplished handling of the fine Neapolitan Courser of State on which he rode to his coronation procession, added to the enthusiasm of his subjects, gathered to watch him pass

Charles II was an accomplished horseman. This was partly due to the tuition he received from the Earl of Newcastle, the horse-loving governor who took charge of the young prince when, aged eight, he was given his own court at Richmond Palace, and who took pains to develop Charles's natural ability. The earl, very sensible of the required gentlemanly attributes of the period, was more than proud of his royal pupil who by the time he was ten could ride and jump the most difficult horses, with or without a saddle, and for whom 'horses goe better than [for] any Italian or French riders'.

The young prince had need of his horsemanship. As the relations of the king and his parliament reached sparking point, the queen was sent to Holland for safety, but the twelve-year-old Charles and his younger brother James accompanied their father in the field through all the first, thrilling phases of the Civil War. The prince's hero was the spirited cavalry commander, his cousin Rupert. When Charles himself was fifteen the king dispatched his son to take command of the royalist forces in the west, an appointment that sounded considerably more exciting and responsible than the rather nominal office it proved to be.

After the tide had turned against the royalists, Prince Charles and his companions fled the country. The next few years were passed in boredom and frustration, with the news from England growing ever worse, and culminating in the tragedy of his father's death which made Charles into an exiled king.

In the eleven years before his restoration in 1660, King Charles's wanderings, in his efforts to regain his kingdom, led him to the ill-advised landing in Scotland which ended with defeat by Cromwell at Worcester, and a desperate ride through the night in the wake of the remnants of his army. In the next six weeks the king, a hounded fugitive in his own kingdom, had numerous hair-raising adventures, including recourse to hiding in the famous oak tree while Crom-well's soldiers searched below. Eventually he set out for Bristol and a hoped-for passage to the Continent, dressed as the servant of a lady, the daughter of a fervent royalist officer, who rode pillion behind him on his horse. The journey was made the more hazardous by their companion, a loyal nobleman attached to the king, who refused to wear a disguise because 'he should look frightfully in it', and by such incidents as when Charles's horse cast a shoe, and while he held up its foot for the blacksmith the man gave him a detailed and accurate description of the clothes and horse of the 'wanted king'. When the Bristol trip proved abortive, the king rode for Brighton where he managed at last to take a ship for France.

The next time King Charles rode through England it was a triumphant journey, acclaimed all the way from Dover through Canterbury and Rochester to London, where 'above twenty thousand horse and foot' brandished their swords and shouted with joy; a journey which culminated in 1661 with another of those magnificent pre-coronation processions, when the king—his dark, handsome features and long, curling black hair set off by 'the rich . . . embroidered suit and cloak', and a dashing, high-crowned hat with its ornamental feather—rode with his nobles from the Tower to Westminster, mounted on a high-stepping Neopolitan Courser of State with nobly arched neck and be-ribboned mane and tail.

All through his reign Charles was to have contending factions to oppose, plots to survive, and crises to overcome.

In 1665 the Great Plague struck London, and as the horses and carts removing the dead proved inadequate for their gruesome task, all those who could fled the hot, noisome streets in panic-stricken crowds. The king too was persuaded to leave Whitehall, and he and his court rode first to Hampton Court and then to Salisbury.

A fire then broke out one night amongst the close-packed wooden buildings in Pudding Lane.

The next day, as the flames leaped from street to street devouring the sun-dried houses of Old London, the king and his brother James rode towards the pall of black smoke and the terrifying roar of the fire from which the throngs of homeless were fleeing.

Despite the help and encouragement of the royal firefighters, the fire raged completely out of control until it had consumed the homes of thousands, whom the king then rode to visit in their wretched, make-shift camp. A gesture of comfort typical of a king who, with all his frailties, combined humanity with a courteous and tolerant nature. And if there were those among the more sober of his citizens to deplore the loose living of their sovereign and his court, for the majority this Merry Monarch proved the most popular of kings. True, his extravagance was a continual bone of contention, but at least the royal finances were depleted as much by the vast sums the king spent annually on importing oriental horses for the royal studs, some of them those 'royal mares' whose progeny helped produce the Thoroughbred, as on the lavish upkeep of his numerous mistresses and illegitimate children. On more than one occasion when the queen and her ladies of honour were decked out to go riding, except for their trailing petticoats in full Cavalier attire, the king might well have been accompanying Lady Castlemaine or another of his favourites on horseback in St James's Park; nor were these the only times when others could be said to have usurped the queen's place.

But by the Restoration the majority of people were as weary of the strictures of the Puritan outlook as they were of the plain dress of the Commonwealth. Life, led by Charles, was frequently once more a matter for colour and fun and laughter, and as many as could thronged to the 'diversions' at which the king delighted to mix 'himself amongst the crowd, [and] allowed every man to speak to him that pleased'. And, as often as not, horses were concerned in some way with these royal pastimes.

When in London the king would rise early to run or ride in the royal parks and—although hawking was going out of favour—when at Winchester he liked to rise at dawn and canter with his red-coated falconers to follow the hawks. The king and his nobles hunted buck with the Royal Pack in the Windsor forests and other regal preserves, and indulged in the new much faster sport of fox-hunting—pursuing a quarry long deemed vermin and to be destroyed by any means, but now elevated to the honour of the chase because so many of the herds of preserved red and fallow deer were dissipated during the Civil War.

Shooting had taken on a new dimension, the hunters no longer creeping up to destroy their birds on the ground, but blazing away at them on the wing from the backs of horses singularly well-inured to the barrage.

The king still hunted hares on horseback, but he had developed

Newmarket from King James's hare-hunting centre to one entirely for racing, the sport which took precedence over all others. And twice a year the king moved into the house at Newmarket, designed for him by Wren, where he could be close by the stables of his cosseted Arabian 'fast-runners'. Then he could spend the days agreeably amongst his jockeys, cheering on his own animals and wagering huge sums on the results of their races, giving cups and jewels in lieu of the bells previously offered as prizes, and sometimes riding a contest himself, not without success.

Those race-horses, like the majority in those times, were all 'bob-tailed', but the animals ridden by the Life Guards (the regiment formed by Charles for the special protection of his own person) had long tails which on ceremonial occasions were tied up with a profusion of ribbons. And a fine sight they made, bestrode by the privates in their round hats with a flourish of white feathers drooping from the back, with their scarlet coats trimmed with gold lace, and thigh-length leather jack-boots to complete the splendid effect; finery which, when the occasion warranted and the horses' tails went unadorned, was changed for defensive cuirasses and iron head-pieces called 'potts', to match the carbines and pistols and swords with which those original Life Guards were armed.

Even towards the end of the seventeenth century the roads were still very bad, but by this time there were stage coaches drawn by teams of six stout horses to carry passengers on local journeys, or to supplement the trains of pack animals by transporting merchandise; in many country districts the housewives were able to welcome a twice-weekly visit by the carrier's cart. It was a source of pride to the king that from some of the larger towns the post was actually brought every day to London, by the post boys who staged the private coaches.

King Charles did not confine his ability with horses purely to riding. He encouraged the developing coach-building business by founding the Company of the Coach and Coach-Harness Makers and, as an accomplished 'Whip' himself, inspired his nobles to drive their own horses as a sport, instead of always relying on the more customary postillions.

Charles II died in 1685 and was succeeded by his brother, who became James II of England and VII of Scotland. James was an unwise man, and proved a foolish monarch who would have done well to take note of the omen of a crown which nearly toppled off his head at his coronation.

The events and temper of his reign might have allowed few opportunities for the king to consider horses in any but the most utilitarian light, but as Duke of York he had been one of the original and most dedicated fox-hunters, and the first of anyone of gentle—

let alone royal—blood to keep a pack of foxhounds. Only weeks before he acceded to the throne he was out with the Royal Buckhounds, he and his suite being led a tremendous chase by a deer that took them through Beaconsfield and Amersham to faraway Oxfordshire.

It seems likely therefore that as king, James still found time for hunting, and certainly horses were occupying his thoughts even in the desperate days when his crown was all but lost. He had already thrown the Great Seal into the Thames, and the army, still undeclared of its intentions, was encamped poised for action at Salisbury; yet there was the king dispatching a message in a letter to his master of the Buckhounds, who was also privy purse, to remind him to send the usual returns of 'the establishment of my horse', and all the latest news from the stable.

Despite the wise and tolerant rule of William and Mary, who succeeded when James II fled the country in 1688, their reign was dominated by long years of war.

It would not have been surprising if William III had found little time for any form of pleasure riding, or for horses other than cavalry chargers. But an Act of Parliament of 1694, to grant licences to the surprising number of 'seven hundred hackney-coaches [that is, four-wheeled carriages] in London and Westminster', was implemented by the king, and he also stipulated that no horse under fourteen hands was to be used in a hackney or stage coach. Whether this was to ensure a faster journey for the passengers, or to prevent cruelty to over-loaded ponies, is not plain.

In those years racing also continued to grow in popularity, and was royally supported, but with the Jockey Club and its governing rules still half a century in the future, little of King William's personal integrity seems to have rubbed off on to the sport of kings. The 'matches' were notoriously crooked, one of the most 'bent' being between an animal belonging to a rich Yorkshireman and that of the king's one-time 'keeper of the running horses'. In this event the network of double-crossings, charges and counter-charges, both before and after the race, and the huge sums of money involved, was so scandalous that it engendered an Act of Parliament to deal specifically with gambling debts of the future.

King William also found time for hunting in Windsor Forest. In connection with the Royal Buckhounds he received a present of one hundred and eight red deer from Germany, and he took the Grand Duke of Tuscany to hunt with the Charlton foxhounds. His horsemanship was such that it was said of him that he refuted the contention that 'the greatest men have not been the best of riders', but it was his misfortune to be killed in a riding accident when coming from Hampton Court.

3 Queen Anne and the Hanoverians

'Outside of a horse . . . inside of a man'

After the death of William III, and about 288 years before her descendant and namesake, Princess Anne, rode her way to become Individual European Eventing Champion, that other Princess Anne, who became a queen, was accorded the title of 'the mightiest huntress of her age'.

In her early married life Queen Anne hunted regularly, both in pursuit of hares and with the Royal Buckhounds. After her accession, in 1702, she was still doing so to an extent that caused Master Pepys to make several censorious notes in his diary about routine admiralty business getting behind-hand because the lord high admiral was absent, hunting.

The queen established the kennels of the Royal Hounds at Ascot, where they remained until the pack was disbanded in the early part of the twentieth century, and she knew every covert and stretch of downland between Winchester and the New Forest like the back of her hand. But as with Elizabeth I, the speed at which even such a dedicated horsewoman conducted her hunting was unlikely to have been very great. As far as the Buckhounds were concerned, it was probably little, if any, faster than the stately pace at which stag-hunting was effected in France, and the queen is unlikely to have attempted much, if anything, in the way of jumping. Fences, a product of the enclosure of common land that was still not completed when George III died, were not very numerous, and were non-existent in the forest hunting. In Queen Anne's era side-saddles lacked a balancing-strap, and the leaping-head was not devised until 1830. Without these two essentials, jumping for lady riders, however intrepid, was virtually impossible.

Frequent (though luckless) child-bearing, ill-health and increased weight eventually precluded the queen from the saddle, but not from her sport. She continued to hunt, driving herself sometimes in a chaise, sometimes in a calash—a kind of gig—following hounds up and down the wide drives cut by royal command in Windsor Forest, and even over bogs especially drained for the purpose.

Hunting was not the only sporting enthusiasm this second daughter of James II inherited from her father, for she took equal pleasure in racing. The name of Queen Anne is always linked with the sport, chiefly because in 1711 the racecourse at Ascot Heath was laid out to her command, and Ascot has been a 'must' for the racing world ever since. She also started running horses at York in 1712, and inaugurated a race for Her Majesty's Gold Cup, run off in four-mile heats, in which her own Pepper was third.

During this reign the import of eastern stallions for the royal studs continued, and twenty-four of Arabian and Barb blood were acquired by the supervisor of the royal race-horses at Newmarket. But none were to have the same influence on the race-horses of the future as the animal that inspired a letter to Queen Anne in 1704.

This epistle, which was to say the least a slight travesty of the truth, was sent by Sheikh Mirza II, and contained a bitter complaint about those of the queen's subjects who had 'foully stolen' the sheikh's priceless Arabian horse. In fact the British consul in Aleppo, a Mr Darley, after handing over the stallion's agreed price of 300 golden sovereigns to the sheikh, had then been denied access to it by order of that wily ruler. Eventually he only gained possession of his purchase through the enterprise of British sailors, who overpowered the guards and brought the horse back to their ship by night.

But if the sheikh was inaccurate in such small essentials, he was correct in the value he set on his horse. The animal, subsequently known as the Darley Arabian, became one of the priceless trio of eastern sires that founded the Thoroughbred.

Queen Anne's enthusiasm for horses did not stop at those used purely for sport. Her interest included the nags and carriage horses connected with everyday riding and driving, and through the queen rules were issued for keeping Hyde Park in proper order for such pastimes: an amenity which enabled the world of royal and high society to put on a fashionable parade each afternoon, riding or driving in the Park with pleasure and in safety—and with the fixed determination both to see and be seen—although the roads in London and the countryside were to remain the haunts of footpads and highwaymen for almost another century.

After Queen Anne's death in 1714, sports connected with horses continued to flourish and expand, but in common with many British ways of life they received small encouragement from the king who succeeded her.

George I was neither an attractive personality nor a popular monarch. He knew little of the country whose crown he wore, and could not even speak the language, but he was over fifty when he acceded to the throne and, not unnaturally, his thoughts and habits remained German rather than English. This trait did at least further the link between the crown and horses, because the king imported Hanoverian animals all through his reign, a royal custom which was enlarged on and continued until well into the twentieth century. On his accession, George I introduced a selection of the famous Creams, together with their scarlet housings of velvet and morocco, that were the horses used on state occasions by the heads of some German states and at the time bred only in studs at Lippe and Gotha. The magnificent Cream stallions were subsequently used on English occasions of the highest state until about 1920. They were bred at Hampton Court, and when replacements became impossible were supplanted first by black state horses, then by bays, and then by the well-known greys.

There is a painting of George I hunting in the Great Park at Windsor where the names of his suite are included, and they are all German, with even the huntsman's name germanized. But in fact, whether his followers were of his own land or of that of his adoption, and for all the string of good horses collected at Windsor for the royal stag-hunting, the king's appearances with the Buckhounds, which were anyway dependent on good weather, were few and far between. And like those of his son, they were confined to meets in the royal parks.

Eight years after his accession in 1727, George II arrived back from a visit to Hanover in the kind of mood when nothing English suited him, including English horses, coachmen and jockeys, the women's clothes and the men's dull political talk; but he was in fact a far better and more anglicized monarch than his father. And he is not the first, nor the last, to have had both temper and health frayed by travelling 'in a violent manner', purely for the pleasure of then bragging about the marvellous speed of his coming.

It was not long before the king appointed a new master of Buckhounds, an official with duties ranging from the obvious one of being accountable for hounds and horses, to distributing king's plates at race-meetings, being responsible for the royal menagerie in Hyde Park (with special reference to the royal tiger), and for feeding the wild turkeys in Bushey Park. Hunting was a favoured royal sport, but it did not amuse George II to arrive home from his travels to discover either his ministers or his court absent at the chase, particularly should they be indulging in fox-hunting. He went so far as to refute the Duke of Grafton's assertion that he fox-hunted for his health, by remarking rudely that no horse could possibly carry the duke's twenty stone weight 'within hearing, much less within sight, of his hounds', but the king himself had fixed hunting days with the Royal Buckhounds.

By royal command Queen Caroline had always to appear on these occasions as well, but she did not venture on horseback. And since she found driving in a chaise behind the hunt for four or five hours a somewhat boring occupation, she undertook to provide horses for Lord Hervey to hunt for the whole of a season—so that he could then ride beside her carriage and entertain her.

There was entertainment of a different sort for the queen, on the hunting day Sir Robert Walpole's horse fell on the road in front of her carriage. Fortunately the king's able statesman, the first prime minister of England, was not hurt, and it seems a little hard that the queen should have 'ordered him to be bled by way of prevention'. There were frequent hunting accidents, and sometimes riders and horses did not escape so well. The lord chamberlain was thrown into a mill-race and nearly drowned, and innumerable hunt servants, lords and ladies of the bedchamber, pages of honour and the lesser gentry who also followed the royal chase, seemed always to be coming to grief, although like their prime minister they apparently survived after undergoing the same sovereign remedy of blood-letting. When one of the royal horses took fright at a swan, and after galloping off became impaled and had to be destroyed, the king was not pleased at being left with an inept if intact groom but deprived of a good horse. Nor were mishaps in the field the only ones to be dreaded. There were so many highwaymen operating in the environs of London that in 1733 the master of the Buckhounds had to take a large armed guard with him when setting out to make arrangements for the coming hunting season.

Two years after George II's grandson came to the throne as King George III, at 5 am on the morning of 24 November 1762, a 'very superb' state coach, later recorded as the most expensive ever built in this kingdom, was delivered to the Royal Mews. Twenty-

The race-horses to be seen at Newmarket during one of George I's infrequent visits were of the eastern blood imported during Queen Anne's reign

His Majesty King George the Thirds New State Coach.

King George III's 'very superb' coach, last used at Queen Elizabeth II's coronation, is on view in all its splendour at the Royal Mews at Buckingham Palace

four feet long, 8 feet 3 inches wide and 12 feet high, gilded all over and magnificently decorated, with the panels painted by Giovanni Cipriani, the coach weighed four tons. At 8 am that morning, eight of the royal Cream stallions were put to it, to try it at a sedate walk round the Mews. It was found eminently satisfactory—just as it has been when used at every coronation since that of George IV, including that of Queen Elizabeth II in 1953.

The Royal Mews where the gold state coach was first tested were those ancient buildings at Charing Cross, north of what is now Trafalgar Square, which the king's grandfather, George II, had had rebuilt in 1732 to a design by William Kent. In the Middle Ages they had been inhabited not by the monarch's horses but by his falcons during their 'mewing' or moult, and it was not until Henry VIII's stables at Lomesbury (Bloomsbury) were burned down that the royal horses took up residence in a royal 'Mewes', and remained there.

In 1762 George III bought Buckingham House, soon to become a Palace, and the stables there were used in addition to those at Charing Cross. But after 1824, when John Nash, commissioned by George IV, redesigned both stabling and coach houses, the Charing Cross site was abandoned. From then those at Buckingham Palace became the Royal Mews, and two years later there was the addition of a Riding House, draughted by the same architect.

For centuries the riding horses that inhabited the Royal Mews were the province of the 'equerries of the crown stable'. When not in attendance on the monarch they were responsible for 'mouthing, managing [manège-ing] and breaking the saddle-horses, and preparing them for the king's riding'. 'Equerry' is a corruption of écurie, French for a stable, and the present-day title of crown equerry, first used in 1854 and bringing with it the appointments of secretary to the master of the horse and superintendent of the Royal Mews, is an obvious contraction of the ancient name. Before then this official was called the gentleman of the horse, and was second-in-command to the master of the horse for whom he could deputize. He was, therefore, and has remained, the senior equerry.

Nowadays the considerable responsibilities of the crown equerry include the royal cars, as well as all the horses except for those in the thoroughbred studs and racing stables. As head of the Royal Mews Department he is concerned with all matters of royal travel by road, as well as with the more spectacular if onerous responsibilities connected with state drives and occasions. However, the modern crown equerry may perhaps consider himself fortunate to have been relieved of some of the duties demanded of his predecessors.

Charles II had eleven equerries who waited on him in turn. The equerry on duty always sat in the leading coach, a sitting target presumably for any trouble that might be lurking by the roadside, and when the king travelled the equerries rode beside his coach, until such time as the custom was discontinued for a while, on account of it 'being more expensive to them than necessary to the sovereign'. Another duty was that the equerry-in-waiting had always to be present to hold the king's stirrup when he mounted his horse; George III seems to have taken a mischievous pleasure in affording as much trouble as he could to the equerry supposed to perform the function, taking a delight in setting out 'before the equerry-in-waiting could possibly be aware of it'. As often as possible he chose the earliest of hours for his excursion, and the worst and most severe weather too would often make the king decide suddenly to set off for a ride. Caught out like this, one equerry was often 'compelled to follow the king down Windsor Hill with scarcely time to pull up his stockings under his boots'. It is scarcely surprising that the £1,000 a year for the chief equerry, and the £750 for the others, proved so inadequate 'to the fatigue and exertions of the post', that the king frequently remarked 'he had fewer applications for the employment of equerry than for any other in his donation'. As a young man the king always rode very hard, so hard in fact that coming from Windsor to London on one occasion his

By the 1970s, coaching was a reviving sport – but few modern whips would care to aspire to the precarious Perch Phaeton, drawn by a team of six, that the future George IV handled with such elegance

companion, the elderly and stout General Keppel, was obliged to forsake the royal presence and go to bed at Turnham Green.

As early as the fifteenth century the then Duke of York was arguing that hunting diverted a man's mind from unwholesome thoughts, and three centuries later a physician was decreeing that 'the best thing for the inside of a man is the outside of a horse'.

George III, a firm believer in both precepts, followed the implied recipe himself, and also prescribed it, not entirely with success, for his son the Prince of Wales, whose thoughts and habits seemed at times in need of diverting into such salutary channels. And so, from Holyrood Day (25 September, which was the start of the season), round to the closing date of the first Saturday in May, the king came out with his Buckhounds on as many of their hunting days— each Tuesday and Saturday, and alternate days during Christmas and Easter weeks—as he could.

The golden age of fox-hunting is said to have been between about 1800 and 1850, its enormous popularity due partly to the fact that, unlike shooting, the sport was not restricted by law to the privileged few. But although it was averred by its supporters that George III would forsake stag-hunting were he to see 'a fox well found', he was not to be shaken in his allegiance to the sport of the royal hounds. Soon after his accession Parliament granted nearly £5,000 a year for their upkeep, and until the insanity that later settled on him precluded it, and despite believing that 'a king and the father of a family should not ride bold', he remained an intrepid follower of the Buckhounds.

True, he once confessed to loving hunting but fearing leaping, and there was a royal pilot to try out the hazards. And when the king decided against following over an obstacle not quite to his liking, he laid yet another burden on his unfortunate equerry, sending that gentleman on willy-nilly after the pilot, while he himself jogged off to find a better spot.

True, too, the hunting was slow, and because of the king's bulk hounds were always being stopped to allow him to catch up. By this time they were hunting carted deer, notable stags and hinds with names like Starlight and Compton, which arrived by deer-cart from the five luxurious deer paddocks at Swinley, to give sport to the king and his followers. Usually each animal ran only a few times in a season, a few of them continued for seven or eight seasons, and there was never any idea that they should be injured. Hounds were held up until the deer was well away—although if the quarry of the day was in a 'mood' it was not uncommon to find it trotting along the road in the middle of the pack—and at the end of the run it would be safely 'taken', with a great fanfare from the French horns then in use to assure hounds the victory was theirs. The deer was then conducted to the first farmhouse available, and bedded down and fed in comfort, before being 'carted' back to the deer paddocks the next day.

The king, in company with the master of the horse, equerries, retainers and any distinguished guests, always arrived at the meet 'critically exact to time', where he too would be greeted with a flourish of French horn music. Then he would exchange his hackney for a hunter, usually either Hobby or Perfection, the two favourites, and after the deer had been sent off, speeded on its way with another musical flourish, the chase was on. And if the pace was not usually very great, the distance covered often was.

After one quick run to Aldermaston, miles beyond Reading, the king in his light blue coat with black velvet cuffs and top-boots buckled up behind, drove home to Windsor in a butcher's cart, conversing learnedly en route with its owner on the respective merits of beef and mutton. On another day the deer, Compton, went away from Ascot Heath at exceptional speed to Windsor Great Park. And here, after some confusion of horsemen, hounds and quarry, the king himself was soon cheering on the hounds after Compton had plunged through the expanse of Virginia Water.

Crowds used to follow the hunt as far as they could on foot, and a great many drove in pursuit, the fashionably turned-out ladies, driven by their escorts in smart yellow post-chaises or gay curricles, adding to the colourful scene. Sometimes the drivers became carried away by the excitement, and on the day when a combination of a mediocre deer and hard-going that lamed the horses had not improved the king's temper, he rebuked a gentleman for driving a phaeton too rashly for his lady passenger's safety—a royal ticking-off which met with general approval.

Once hounds had been drawn off and the deer taken, the king and his entourage usually made for the nearest town to hire post conveyances for taking them back to Windsor. This often entailed a drive in darkness, but the king was always guarded by two yeoman prickets who rode on either side of his carriage, each armed with a brace of horse pistols carried all day with the hunt by a couple of boys on horseback. On several occasions it was eight or nine in the evening before the king, tired, content, and famished arrived back at the castle. But between 1788-9, when the king suffered the first bout of the physical and mental illness which eventually destroyed him, there were to be no more homecomings, late or not, after a satisfying run with hounds. Eventually poor 'Farmer George's' blue hunting coat and the top-boots were put away for ever.

In a lucid moment during his relapse in 1801, the king sat down to dine *tête-à-tête* with the Prince of Wales—a rare enough happening

Above: George III, the King who even during his distressing bouts of illness dearly loved to see a fine horse with a skilled rider, reviewing the Honourable Artillery Company

Below: The buildings near Trafalgar Square, originally inhabited by the royal falcons in moult, where Henry VIII housed his horses. After 1824 these stables were abandoned in favour of the present Royal Mews at Buckingham Palace

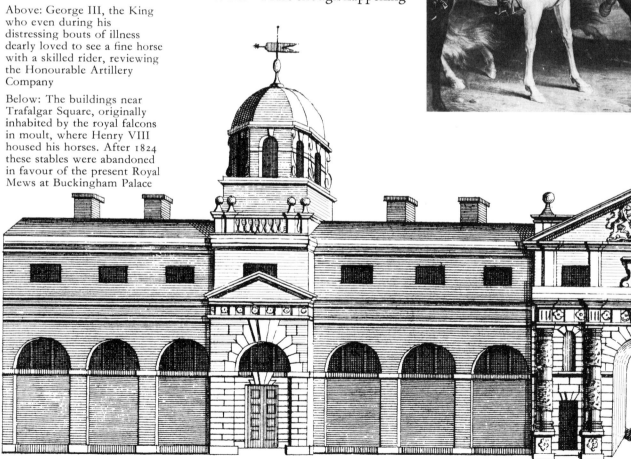

for a father and son who had been at odds since 'Prinny' was a boy —and during the evening he insisted that the prince accept one of the prized Cream Hanoverian horses. After this the poor king's conversation became very wild, but as the Prince of Wales was an accomplished horseman with an abiding interest in horseflesh, the gift would have been much appreciated.

One of the first portraits of the prince shows him trotting through a meadow on his pony with two dogs at his heels, and when he was a young man his proudest boast was that he rode from London to Brighton and back in a day, a distance of 108 miles covered in ten hours. 'Prinny' loved to try out any good-looking hack or hunter that a dealer cared to produce. And since he luckily possessed a competent style of riding—and a seat so elegant that even his skin-tight pantaloons remained unwrinkled—he was happy to show off the best of the animals to the admiration of the company assembled at Carlton House or the Pavilion at Brighton. His favourite hacks were Tobacco Stopper, and Tiger, which he was warned was 'short of bone' and might stumble, a caution the prince ignored since he believed that 'Tiger disdains to fall down!'

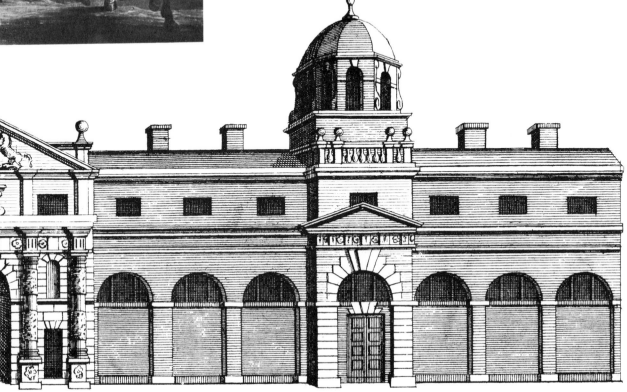

Another source of much pride was Prinny's skill as a Whip. He 'reckoned it pretty good driving' to have covered twenty-two miles in two hours at a trot with a phaeton and four, as indeed it was. As his love of Brighton and the Marine Pavilion he built there developed, many were the days that found the Prince of Wales on the road down from London, with some lady of quality who might or might not be the latest of his loves, driving that sporting conveyance of the time, a Perch phaeton. This was an elegant but precarious vehicle, dangerous enough with a pair of horses, let alone the six-in-hand that the prince sometimes affected for Ascot, aided only by a postillion riding the near-side leader; nevertheless even that he handled with considerable dash and skill.

Before he grew 'too enormously large' for it to be feasible, the Prince of Wales hunted as enthusiastically as his father, and was often to be met returning from the chase, 'with all the maids of honour on horseback, tired and hot' following on behind. Between 1788 and 1793, when he was living at Kemshot, he had his own pack of staghounds, and this too was the era of a hunter that was, according to his royal owner, 'not only the finest but the best horse he ever saw'. The prince paid a very high figure for this animal, so it was as well that the best runs he ever witnessed were 'from the back of his dear Curricle'.

The prince also hunted with the Royal Buckhounds, but regrettably it was too often the king rather than the hounds that provided his son's sport, as he and some boon companion derided 'Farmer George's' unfashionable attire, and mocked his slow-paced horses and leisurely pursuit of the deer. In 1813, after the break-up of the historic Charlton Hunt, Prinny, by then prince regent, was given the Goodwood hounds by the Duke of Richmond. Their arrival at Ascot, and the appointment as first whipper-in of a man who was to become a famous huntsman, marked the beginning of a new style of stag-hunting. With faster hounds it was an altogether speedier sport, less concerned with the former picturesque ritual, and without the prolonged and noisy accompaniment of musical venery produced by the French horns, for which a modern shaped horn carried only by the huntsman was substituted.

Maybe if the prince had limited his interests in horseflesh to the handsome hacks he rode with such grace in the London parks and along the Steine at Brighton; or to his harness horses and assortment of fashionable vehicles, and to furthering his undoubted expertise as a whip; or to his hunters and hunting, of which the king heartily approved, he might have avoided the worst of the monumental debts that were a continual source of friction with his father. There would still have been such extravagances as the luxurious stabling for fifty-four horses, and the Riding House with its huge central

Opposite: Until the scandal concerning his jockey, the Prince of Wales was as familiar a figure at Newmarket (top) as he was at Ascot, Lewis and Brighton (centre) racecourses. But even with Newmarket eschewed, his racing expenses reached appalling proportions, far exceeding anything he spent on his famed Marine Pavilion at Brighton (bottom), or on the beauties of the day he entertained there

cupola at the Marine Pavilion, and indeed everything connected with His Royal Highness's establishments, but the losses on racing might have been avoided. However, the prince and his entourage were as well known on the Brighton and Lewes racecourses as they were at Ascot and Newmarket, as well as venues such as the Salisbury track where the prince once drove Lady Banfylde all day on the course in a borrowed phaeton, although she was 'grown fat, old and ugly, but His Royal Highness is not noted for his taste in females'. His racing of course encompassed the many who were only too happy to help swell the vast load of royal gambling debts.

By 1784 the king, unhappily not for the last time, was requesting the head of the prince's household to try and ascertain the exact amount of his eldest son's liabilities. The estimated results were appalling, and included the 'amazing expense' of £31,000 a year for the upkeep of His Royal Highness's racing stables, with the cost liable to go up 'beyond all kind of calculation whatever'. But the outlay on race-horses and their upkeep was not the only trouble connected with the prince's association with the turf. Although it was never proved, and the prince himself was blameless, there was a scandal concerning his horse Escape, and Chiffney, a well-known jockey he had engaged as 'rider for life' in 1790. The prince was so angry at the implications that he forswore Newmarket then, and never patronized the course again. But there was still suspicion and he was told that if he retained Chiffney, no gentleman would allow a horse to compete in the same race. A year later the prince's stud was sold at Tattersalls and it was 1826 before he returned to the turf.

George III died in 1820, and the Prince of Wales succeeded as King George IV, after nine years as regent. At the time his unpopularity was as much due to his appalling extravagance as to his treatment of his wife, but typically the crowning could scarcely have been more lavish, costing in the region of £238,238, an immense sum for those days. Amongst the items was £118 18 6, charged by the master of the horse for an animal ridden by the King's Champion, who performed his duties at the banquet in Westminster Hall for the last time.

The coronation banquet of George III had been enlivened by the incident of the lord high steward's horse, a sagacious animal which had been painstakingly taught to leave the royal presence backwards, but which got its wires a little crossed and on the actual occasion persisted instead on entering the banqueting hall in reverse. No such unrehearsed light relief was provided for that of George IV, and indeed the temper of the people was such that after the banquet the royal carriages were forced to make a wide detour to avoid the crowds. The entourage had to return along mean streets which included a condemned and dangerous bridge over a deep canal, where the 'planks cracked, shook [and] bent' as horses and conveyances edged their way across.

When he succeeded to the throne the new king was already sixty years old, and obese. Two years after his accession he was writing to congratulate the new huntsman of his one-time pack of staghounds, and expressing the hope that he would 'get them so fast that they will run away from everybody', but the king's personal hunting was confined to the occasional visit to see hounds in kennel. In the remaining years of his life riding, too, was out of the question, but the king was still to be seen on occasions driving his pony phaeton with all the old dash, a yeoman pricket acting as outrider and two grooms behind.

In 1791, when he was still Prince of Wales, the king once organized a stag hunt for the entertainment of the many distinguished French *émigrés* from the Revolution who were staying at Kemshot. Included in the field was Prince William, his younger brother, who was to become the Duke of Clarence and eventually succeeded to the throne. At the time William was a midshipman at Portsmouth, and his hunting that day finished up in a deep ditch which he and his hired pony failed to negotiate. He was to run a horse at Goodwood within six weeks of the death of George IV, and he was to win the Derby twice. Apart from these victories that hunting mishap was perhaps symptomatic of the fact that horses, apart from their utilitarian aspect, were never to play quite the same part in the life of William IV, either before or after his accession, as they did with the other members of the House of Hanover. William was a sailor. As a young man he had served in the royal navy for ten years, only returning to England at short intervals until, by the express wish of both his father and Parliament, his commission was terminated. As a typical member of his profession, he was little interested in horses, although they did further his standing on that occasion in 1831 when the king was requested to recommend the immediate dissolution of Parliament. 'It was noticed that His Majesty proceeded at a faster rate than usual, in his eagerness to carry out the wishes of his people'; but the spanking trot which brought the king to the House ahead of schedule was in fact unintentional: the king's decision to depart on his mission forthwith had left no time even to plait the Cream stallions' manes before setting out, and both coachman and horses were already flurried when the team shied at a saluting ensign and took off, despite the efforts of their driver and the epithets he shouted at the guardsman.

Contrary to expectations, William IV did keep the royal stud at Hampton Court up to a high standard, and there were remonstrances from Parliament as well as from the Jockey Club when the horses were sold after the king's death in 1837.

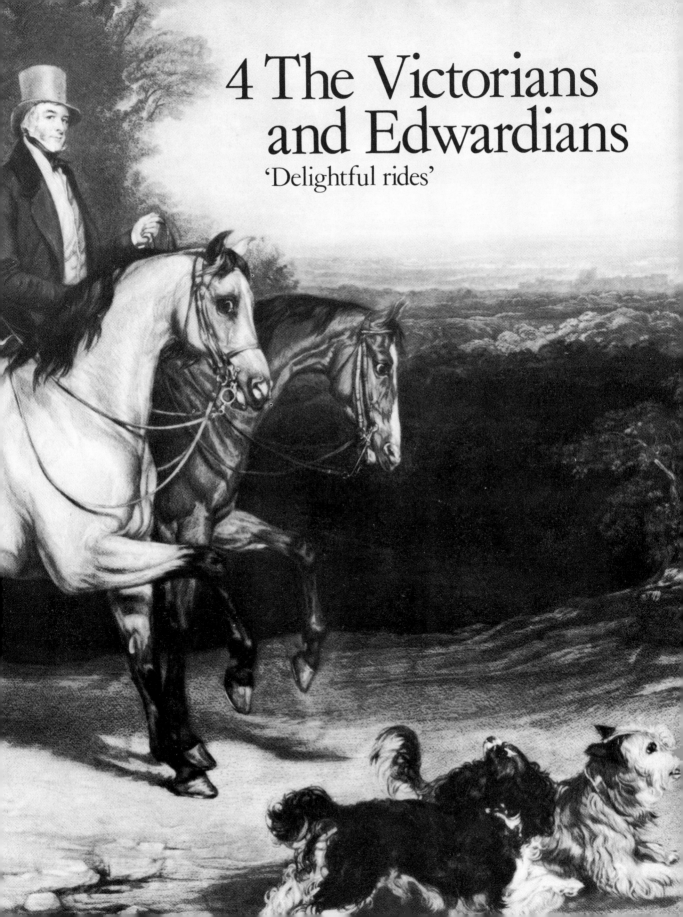

4 The Victorians and Edwardians

'Delightful rides'

Previous pages: The young
Queen Victoria riding with
Lord Melbourne in Windsor
Park

On Sunday, 14 October 1832, the thirteen-year-old Princess
Victoria, daughter of George III's son the Duke of Kent, was
galloping over a green field with her mother, the duchess.
Later that day she noted in her Journal that: 'Rosa went at an enormous
rate; she literally *flew* . . .', and there is more of this pony the next
year when the princess and her companions went riding in the park,
where they 'cantered a good deal' and 'little Rosa went beautifully!!'

All through her long life this princess, who became queen and
was to reign longer than any British monarch to date, was to find
great joy in her horses, and until age and family affairs precluded
her from the saddle every venture on horseback was noted as 'a
delightful ride'.

Horses of every kind were of course almost as much part of
Princess Victoria's 'scene' as they were of her ancestors', and were to
remain so throughout her life. 1834, the year she was fifteen, was
when coaching was in its prime, and although the stage and mail
coaches began to be superseded by steam three years after Victoria
came to the throne, it was 1842 before the queen and her consort

were to venture by train. It was a memorable journey from Windsor to Paddington, which the prince hoped would be 'not so fast next time' but which the queen found an agreeable change from the rocking of royal carriages, driven at speed to avoid the gathering of boisterous crowds.

Innovation might be in the air, but for almost all the Victorian era London would still echo to the unchallenged clatter of iron-shod hooves and the rumble of iron-rimmed wheels.

It was small wonder that in such a horse-dominated world the young Princess Victoria should ride well. But to those only familiar with pictures of the staid, bereaved queen of later years, setting out on Lochnagar or another of her beloved deer ponies to explore the Scottish Highlands, but always led sedately by the kilted John Brown, the pace and extent of her riding in the early years is an unexpected delight.

As it happened Princess Victoria did little riding between her sixteenth birthday and the momentous occasion, two years later, when she left Kensington Palace to take up residence at Buckingham

The elegant grey animals with which Queen Victoria loved to take the air around the grounds at Windsor, were known as the Windsor Greys – a name still given to the grey state carriage horses in the Royal Mews

The times spent amongst the mountains and lochs of Scotland, where sure-footed Highland ponies enabled Victoria to accompany her husband on his sporting excursions, were some of the happiest of the Queen's life

Palace as Queen of England. The days were filled with the lessons that by then held more significance, with meeting people of distinction, with illness, and with trying hard to learn what 'a queen *ought* to be'. And despite the king's rage and her daughter's reluctance, the duchess insisted on yet another of those journeyings around England which King William alluded to sarcastically as 'royal progresses'. There was no driving accident that time, as there had been at Hastings in the previous year—when a horse with a leg over the traces brought the pair drawing the princess's landau down in a kicking tangle on the road; or as there was so nearly to be in 1837, when a near-hurricane almost swept the postboys from the horses' backs as the royal party left Canterbury, and flying corn-stacks and chimney pots, uprooted trees, and the eventual terror of the horses going downhill into Chatham, necessitated a stay overnight at Rochester. But if there were none of these excitements on the long drive north and back, there was heat, and dust, and headache, and backache, and Victoria was thankful to be home again. For though she 'liked some of the places very well', she was 'much tired by the long journeys and great crowds', and the impossibility of being able to 'travel like other people, quietly and pleasantly. . . .'

Princess Victoria acceded to the throne in 1837, and within days had summoned her master of the horse and asked him to provide, immediately, six chargers for her to review her troops. This was to be a military duty she was to perform with obvious pleasure; wearing the ribbon of the Garter over her dark blue habit with red collar and cuffs, the colours of the Windsor uniform ('which all my gentlemen wear'), and riding Leopold, who was 'very handsomely harnessed', the young queen made an enchanting picture as she set off for the Home Park at Windsor, on a day towards the end of September in that same year. She was attended by a little page in the same uniform, on a pony accoutred to match the royal charger, and had an escort of the Lancers, with the duchess and others of the court also on horseback, and the remainder of the ladies and gentlemen driving in carriages behind.

The 1st Regiment of Life Guards, the Grenadier Guards, and a squadron of the Lancers were drawn up on the parade ground, and after acknowledging the regiments' salute, 'by putting my hand to my cap . . . and was much admired for my manner of doing so', the queen and her G.O.C. escort, surprisingly, *cantered* up to the lines and rode along them. Despite bands playing in its face her horse Leopold behaved imperturbably, as he was to do throughout the ceremony after the queen had again cantered back to her position.

Victoria loved that review. She felt that, 'like a man', she could lead her troops into battle as monarchs did of old, and the parade was the chief topic of conversation when she changed horses and habit back at the castle and rode out in company, with Lord Melbourne beside her, for an hour and a half's relaxation.

The ceremony was repeated the next year, when it was enlivened even more for the queen by Leopold quickening his canter up to and away from the lines she was inspecting, to the extent where his rider thought he might be running away, but she obviously enjoyed it.

Although both military occasions were a great success, the queen did not perhaps get the opportunity to try out all of her 'six chargers' in the following years. She was, anyway, a great one for favourites amongst her horses—for all the number of animals housed in the Royal Mews, time and again it was to be the same pair that brought the royal carriage to meet the queen at Paddington station, the same team that took her for her airing in the Park. Then, at the military review at Hyde Park in 1838, much to her disappointment, the queen had been advised to drive instead of riding. In later years this was an accepted practice, but at the time it was felt to be an error of judgement by Lord Melbourne who underestimated the impact, on troops and spectators alike, made by the fascinating spectacle of the young queen on horseback.

Lord Melbourne, the great Whig statesman who was to become

R.O.H.—D

Victoria's prime minister and was her confidante, guardian, guide and best friend all through the early years of her reign, had plenty of opportunity for admiring his sovereign in the attractive black velvet habit, top hat and veil she wore for everyday riding excursions.

Like other ministers he was often included, and then usually in the place of honour by her side, when the queen and her cavalcade of thirty or more set off—sometimes on rides that appear almost marathons by modern standards. One day it would be out through the gardens at Buckingham Palace by the gate on to Constitution Hill, and into the rattle of the omnibuses and carts and carriages of the noisy streets. Then round the park by the water and to within four miles of Harrow, before returning by Willesden Field and Kilburn, down the Edgeware Road and Connaught Place, and into the Park again at Cumberland Gate to end the three-hour trip with a gallop back to Hyde Park Corner.

Some days the queen would be riding her dear, sure-footed Tartar, a little dark-brown horse with a springy action and delightful manners, and the animal which took part in a 'charming ride' when they galloped at least three miles without once pulling up. When the outing took in twenty miles through Acton to Hanwell and home by Castle Hill, this time it was the turn of Uxbridge, another favourite, full of spirit yet the 'most charming, delightful, quiet horse possible'.

In October 1837 Lord Melbourne had been of the royal party that rode all round Virginia Water, and then cantered most of the way home on the hottest of evenings. In the previous weeks he had been out riding with the queen most days, opportunities he took for discussing everything from politics and the state of the country to the most sophisticated social chit-chat and viewpoints of the age, while his young companion gradually grew from girlhood to maturity. Her minister did not however attend the queen's sessions in the Riding House when she tried out various horses, and he was not present at that moment when her admiration for her horse, Monarch, was considerably increased. This occasion was when the queen was riding in Queen Anne's Walk and a sudden terrifying flash of lightning and clap of thunder directly overhead sent her Aunt Louise's horse plunging off at full gallop. Monarch, startled but still mannered, remained where he was, and fortunately the Queen of the Belgians' horse stopped when it came to a hill; while, with the toughness characteristic of the Victorian lady equestrian, its rider was 'not in the *least* frightened but only "quite ashamed"!'

Lord Melbourne was with the queen, and possibly wished he was not, on the day she fell off. They were riding on ahead of the 'cavalcade' when Uxbridge, upset by the departure of the queen's

other companion, her Uncle Leopold, King of the Belgians, swerved so violently that its rider slipped off sideways. Her poor minister was 'quite frighted and turned quite pale', but the queen, neither hurt, put out nor frightened, but only 'astonished and amused', at once remounted and cantered home.

Lord Melbourne always considered the young queen's riding activities to be a very good thing. As he commented: 'It [riding] gives a feeling of ease the day one has·done with Parliament', and after marriage Victoria continued with the sport that gave her such joy.

Her husband, Prince Albert, grew up in a little Schloss set deep in the heart of a forest outside Coburg. There, with all the sights and scents of the countryside on his doorstep, he became involved in the pattern of country life as a matter of course. Gardening, wild life, riding and hunting were pursuits as natural as the music and art included amongst his talents, and for one as elegant in movement as he was in looks, it was inevitable that the prince consort should be as accomplished a horseman as he was a dancer.

His adoring wife had many opportunities for admiring Albert's skill as he tried out the royal horses in the Riding Houses at Buckingham Palace and Windsor Castle; she watched him return

from hunting, and at the march past at a military review there was the prince at the head of his regiment, riding by his queen at the salute with his eyes fixed on hers.

When the queen was not engaged with one or other of the numerous infants, they rode together as a leisure pastime, in London, at Windsor, and at their 'retreat', Osborne House in the Isle of Wight. Often the chosen horses would be a pair of Arabs, the grey Tajar which belonged to the prince, and the chestnut Hammon, presented to the queen by the King of Prussia in 1844, which frequently carried her during the next seventeen years.

When they discovered that other haven, the pretty little castle in the old Scottish style, on the site of the present Balmoral Castle which was then built and finished in 1856, there were lovely informal excursions on deer ponies into the hills. Expeditions when Albert could shoot while Victoria sketched, and where the queen felt 'so safe' on Fyvie or another of her loved Highland animals as, led by the head ghillie they scrambled up over the rocky tracks, 'never making a false step'.

As soon as they were old enough the children were taught to ride as a matter of course. The Prince of Wales, perched on the deer-saddle and led by a ghillie, with another walking alongside for

In old age, the Queen still enjoyed her outings. Left: In Dublin in 1900, and (overleaf) in Grasse, a year later, the horse-power of each smart turn-out was provided by a donkey

emergencies, accompanied his parents on some of the early deer-stalking treks. When he was only seven there was an anxious occasion in Windsor Park when his pony ran away, a *contretemps* which was, however, kept from his father who had a horror of accidents. But in the days of horse transport no aversion could prevent the various mishaps which occurred, even in royal circles, when riding or driving. Once the queen was tipped out of her pony-chair when it ran up against an ant-hill; another time she had to be pulled out of her carriage into the mud when it overturned at a meet. She, as usual, found both incidents amusing, but it was a different matter when the misadventure involved Albert. Amongst other incidents he also had a fall when hunting, and a very narrow escape when the royal team bolted and the prince only just jumped clear before horses and carriage crashed into a wagon held up at a level-crossing.

Prince Albert died in 1862, and that was the moment the light went out for Queen Victoria. Frightened by her prolonged melancholia, someone tried the expedient of bringing a favourite Highland pony down from Balmoral to Osborne, with the ghillie John Brown to lead it and remain permanently as 'the queen's highland servant'. Time contrived to restore the queen's spirits to a degree, but from then on the royal ventures on horseback seem always to have been taken with someone—until his death in 1883 with John Brown, leading the pony. And always her driving expeditions also included him either at the pony's head or on the box beside her coachman.

The grey 'ponies' (despite the fact that by size they were horses) which drew the queen's carriage around the grounds at Windsor, initiated the name of the Windsor Greys, the title by which the famous state carriage horses are often known today. When old age at last crept up on Victoria, in her white cap and black bombazine dress with white at throat and wrists—seemingly more diminutive yet her dignity still matchless—the invalid carriage favoured for taking the air at Osborne or Balmoral was drawn by a small shaggy pony as venerable as herself. When the era ended, the queen had herself already ensured that the horses drawing the gun-carriage bearing her coffin to the Albert Memorial Chapel at Windsor should not be of the plumed 'black brigade' favoured for Victorian funerals. An army team of the Royal Artillery were to have the sad honour of taking the queen to her rest, but in the event, after one of the horses had snapped its traces, it was the guard of sailors which dragged the gun-carriage to bring the queen home.

Queen Victoria was dead, a century and a way of life was finished, and, though no one could visualize the speed with which the world would change, the day of the horse in its true utilitarian sense was almost over too.

Opposite above: Alexandra, the captivating Princess of Wales from Denmark, who loved to ride and hunt – a pastime for ladies of which Queen Victoria did not approve. From an early age she involved her children in 'horse interest'

Below: Her sons, Prince Albert Victor, who died in 1892, and Prince George, who became King George V, with their ponies in 1873

Overleaf: The utility role of the horse, as known from time immemorial, faded quickly with the end of the Victorian era. But this carriage used by the Queen on a visit to Newport in 1897 is still in royal use today, and is drawn by much the same type of horse

Driving is a different art to riding, equally attractive to its exponents. There is a tradition of royal whips, illustrated here by Queen Victoria (right), her granddaughters, the Princesses Victoria and Maud of Wales (opposite above), and Princess Louise, Duchess of Fife, who is driving her father Albert Edward, Prince of Wales (below)

As Prince and Princess of Wales, the new King Edward and his lovely queen consort, Alexandra, shared a common interest in horses which they never lost. But as early as 1899 there was Edward driving as passenger with Lord Montagu of Beaulieu in a 12-h.p. Daimler. Soon cars were included in the 'royal stable', and from 1901 onwards three automobiles with chauffeurs to match were sent in advance when the king went off to Biarritz or Marienbad. Even Alexandra, whose dashing expertise as a 'Whip' began with a goat and go-cart, and whose fine horsemanship sprang from idyllic childhood summers spent at the Bernstorff hunting-lodge with her brothers and sisters and a donkey—even she was enthusiastic over the new form of locomotion. By 1901 she too was declaring motoring to be one of her greatest pleasures.

Despite the horrifying curriculum that had been forced on the unstudious-minded Prince of Wales by his father, it was natural that riding had been encouraged, both privately and in public. Edward had attended the ceremony in Hyde Park when Queen Victoria distributed the first Victoria Crosses, won in the Crimean War, mounted on his pony and wearing the kilt; a somewhat unconventional riding attire which was also to appeal to his great-great-grandson, Prince Andrew, about a hundred years later when, aged

At the end of the nineteenth century, riding was still a social accomplishment – and certainly royalty was no exception. Left to right: Princess Maud, Prince Albert Victor, Alexandra, Princess of Wales, Prince George

four, he insisted on the kilt for riding his Shetland along the Balmoral tracks.

To natural riding ability the Prince of Wales had brought an abundance of 'nerve'. One of his worst falls was occasioned when his horse pecked at a stiff fence that was only jumped for a wager, and the inevitable tosses he took out hunting never dimmed his readiness to gallop on and tackle any type of obstacle.

Queen Victoria's personal involvement with hunting had been confined to a few occasions like that of 1832, when she 'walked to see the hunt' with her governess, and to her first and only appearance at a meet of the Royal Buckhounds in 1874, with a visit to the kennels a year later. But during the eighteenth and nineteenth centuries fox-hunting was looked on as the democratic sport. The queen urged her eldest son—Bertie as they called him—to emulate its principles and 'do away a little with the *exclusive* character of shooting', because much as she disliked hunting on account of the danger, it was this aspect that made it so popular.

Edward may possibly have applied this advice towards the guest guns who accompanied him when he rode his shooting pony to the beats at Sandringham, but although he did much during his

The lovely Alexandra, Princess of Wales, was an accomplished horsewoman and loved to ride. When rheumatic fever stiffened her right knee, she overcame the difficulty by moving the pommel to the off-side of her saddle

life to democratize the monarchy, as Prince of Wales and as king his outlook still remained essentially conservative.

After marriage the Prince and Princess of Wales both gave themselves plenty of opportunities for imbibing the broadening influence of hunting the fox. In his teens, Edward was said to have 'rode boldly and well' over a stiff country when out with the South Oxfordshire, and he hunted from both Cambridge and Oxford. By the 1860s, and despite increased weight, the Prince of Wales was sampling the sport offered by some of the 'cream' of the shires, the Belvoir and the Quorn, and nine years earlier had a fall when hunting over heavy country with the East Sussex. That day his wife had driven him to Sidley Green to collect his horse, a practice which, as an excellent if somewhat reckless Whip, she sometimes indulged when not hunting herself.

In their early married days Alexandra's fixed intention of hunting, a pastime not common with Victorian ladies, met with horror and disapproval from her mother-in-law. As became usual on the few occasions when they clashed, the princess wore down the royal opposition by yielding for a while and then continuing happily on her own way. It was little time before the attractive and

lovely figure of the Princess of Wales, wearing the apron skirt that
was the new vogue, a slender fitted jacket which accentuated her
tiny waist, and the becoming top-hat with its knot of veiling that set
off her features, was again to be seen out with her husband enjoying
a day's sport with the West Norfolk. At least once it was with Mr
Bircham's Harriers at Fitcham Abbey, and when the severe weather
of the 1865 winter at last let up, the royal couple had a day out from
Osborne House with the Isle of Wight Foxhounds. Sometimes the
meet was at their home, Sandringham House, when the field num-
bered more than five hundred, with a crowd of carriages to follow
as well. And it was on one of these occasions, when the princess was
also hunting, that a horse out of control charged straight into the
prince, knocking him out of the saddle and sending his hunter off at
full gallop: one of the inevitable mishaps, like the day when his horse
'seemed not to understand the big banks and ditches' and gave its
royal rider a couple of falls, which the Prince of Wales took in his
stride. Soon it would be recorded that 'although His Royal Highness
is not as light as he was, he rides with undiminished pluck. . . .'

The prince also had good fun in the earlier years with the
queen's hounds—the Royal Buckhounds—although perhaps it
was more for the tradition and idea of a royal pack, and as a
ride and a pastime, than for the sport. But there were several notable
runs, if few to beat that on the day, 2 March 1868, when the meet
was at Denham Court. A strong deer took them on a run past
Pinner to the foot of Harrow Hill, then up over the top and down
into the 'Duckpuddle Fields' and so on to Wormwood Scrubbs—
where misfortune overtook the Duc de Chartres, stuck with his
horse in a bog, a wire fence round its legs. They eventually took the
deer at Paddington goods station, and afterwards the entire field
accompanied the Prince of Wales home to Marlborough House,
'riding through Hyde Park and down Constitution Hill in hunting
dress'.

Hunting of a rather different kind was enjoyed by the Prince
of Wales when he went on his Indian tour in the autumn of 1875.
He needed all the riding ability he possessed on the day he was on
horseback and elected to face a wild elephant. When it charged, and
the encircling horsemen had to gallop for their lives, there were
some anxious moments for the prince's Indian host who was
responsible for the safety of the heir to the English throne. In the
ensuing attack, designed to keep the elephant fully occupied in the
open until the advent of the tame fighting elephants, the prince had
several times to put his splendid Arabian horse to top speed to carry
him out of danger. When the elephant was eventually captured, it
is nice to be able to record that at the prince's request it was then
given its freedom once more.

Unlike her great-great-
grandmother, the Queen does
not review her troops on
horseback, but each year she
takes the salute at the
Trooping the Colour

In the Inner Court at Buckingham Palace, after taking the salute, the Queen rewards the police horse that has acted as her mannered charger and so added to the splendour of this colourful military ceremony

Above: Princess Anne's
interest in horse shows began
at an early age

Right: Inevitably his naval
career now restricts Prince
Charles's polo playing, but
whenever possible he seeks
relaxation in the sport in
which he shows so much
promise

Overleaf: Before school sports
and games provided alternative
attractions, the Queen's younger
sons sometimes joined royal
family riding parties. The Queen
with Princess Anne and Prince
Andrew, then aged four, in
the grounds at Sandringham

Above: In a life of exacting duty, horses provide the Queen with the opportunity to 'get away from it all'.

Right: Helping with the polo ponies between chukkas at Smith's Lawn, Windsor, was always one of Anne's prerogatives

Overleaf: A Dressage test, the first phase of an Event or Horse Trial, may not look very exacting to the uninitiated, but it requires good riding, co-ordination with one's horse, and a lot of concentration.

Left: Princess Anne with Columbus

The cross-country phase, more than four miles long with a miscellany of really big jumps in the top-notch Events, calls for a bold horse, a courageous rider and mutual confidence.

Right: Princess Anne with Doublet at Burghley

Above and opposite: As a boy Mark Phillips rode and competed at Pony Club level. When he joined the army these interests were furthered and he was soon prominent in the Eventing world. He won the Three-Day Event at Badminton in 1971 and '72, and at Burghley in 1973 on a borrowed horse of only one week's acquaintance. In 1974 he won Badminton on the Queen's Columbus

Overleaf: In the days when Prince Philip played polo, visiting the ponies in his yard (left) and practising on the lawn at Windsor gave him opportunities to unwind quite apart from the actual games and matches. Driving is his sport now, and the Prince does it with his usual thoroughness. Much practice at Windsor and Sandringham helped him to graduate quickly from driving a single horse to a pair, and then to the ultimate in the whip's art, a four-in-hand

The young Princess Victoria drove with King William and his queen, with an escort of eight other carriages, to Ascot races in 1834, and a year later was present on the course at Tunbridge Wells to see Mr Pegg's horse, Little-Thought-Of, win the Kent and Sussex Stakes. As queen she was usually present at Ascot, and once at the Derby, and she maintained a successful breeding-stud of Thoroughbred racehorses at Hampton Court. But the turf was not her *métier*, and she could scarcely approve her Bertie's preoccupation with the sport of kings, even though, together with the big yacht racing which was another enthusiasm, it brought him a lot of popularity.

For the Prince of Wales, barred by his mother for at least ten years after the prince consort's death from any share in the work of the monarchy, or anything much that might help prepare him for his eventual responsibilities, it was not unnatural that racing, in all its aspects, as well as other less desirable facets of the social scene, should help to fill his days.

The Prince of Wales's racing colours—the purple, gold braid, scarlet sleeves and black velvet cap with gold fringe in which the queen's jockey rides today—first appeared under Jockey Club rules at Newmarket in 1877, for a match between the prince's Arab horse and another, a part-bred, that established the superior speed of Thoroughbred blood. His name first appeared amongst the list of winning owners in 1886.

Like any other owner, the prince's successes fluctuated from season to season, but his great horse Persimmon, the almost legendary animal whose huge bronze statue still dominates the Royal Sandringham Stud, won the 1896 Derby for its royal owner. It followed that triumph up in the next year by winning the Eclipse Stakes and the Gold Cup at Ascot, and in 1900, Diamond Jubilee, Persimmon's full brother and a horse of uncertain temperament, gained another royal Derby. In addition, this animal won the Two Thousand Guineas, the Eclipse Stakes and the St Leger—crowning a wonderful and almost unparalleled season which began with His Royal Highness's steeplechaser, Ambush II, winning the Grand National.

Nine years later the king scored a full-house once more, taking the Greenham Stakes, the Two Thousand Guineas, the Derby, the St James's Palace Stakes at Ascot, Goodwood's Surrey Stakes and the Free Handicap at Newmarket, all with another famous horse called Minoru. By 5 May 1910 the king was gravely ill, and only a few hours after hearing of the success of his filly, Witch of the Air, he died.

Both before and after she became queen, Alexandra took an interest in her husband's race-horses and occasionally attended some

Opposite: Horses play an important role in the lives of many of the royal family, and possibly Princess Anne has obtained most from her absorbing hobby

Overleaf: Albert Edward, Prince of Wales, in the uniform of the 10th Hussars, 1897 (left), and in less military attire (right), after he had been out riding with Tsarevitch Alexander of Russia (right)

Both as Prince of Wales and as
King, Edward VII was a keen
racing man. He was the proud
owner of the great Persimmon
whose many successes were as
popular with the racing crowds
as they were with its owner
(right). Above and far right:
King Edward with Persimmon
at Newmarket in 1897 and
1885

of the classic meetings, but her delight in horses was a much more personal one, and the circumstances of her life intensified this outlook. Riding meant a great deal to her, and after a serious and painful bout of rheumatic fever early in 1867 left her with a permanently stiff right knee, it seemed she might never be able to ride again; a grim prospect for someone who delighted to gallop a horse, to dance and skate, and to lead an athletic outdoor life.

The princess was still crippled when she left to try the baths at Wiesbaden in August that year. But it was determination more than any spa treatment that eventually enabled her to get back on to horseback, accommodating her stiff leg by moving the pommel to the off-side of her saddle and sitting in the less orthodox position.

It was sad that this illness also stirred up the hereditary deafness to which Princess Alexandra was prone. The passing years then brought increasing isolation in a silent world, and gradually she withdrew more often to the haven of home and children where the countryside, dogs and horses took over from most of her former social interests.

While her husband was still alive there were to be many informal and gay house parties at Sandringham, where horses and hunting played a large part in the advocated amusements, and the conversation often touched on the buying or selling of one of the Princess of Wales's numerous horses. And when the princess accompanied her husband abroad, her letters to their young sons usually had at least a reference to her favourite animals—once it was to the little Indian pony that had walked all the way upstairs to her dressing-room, and down again, just 'like a Christian'.

When appendicitis struck the king two days before his coronation, the queen deputized for him at a huge military review. She was always nervous at big public functions and on that day had to combat acute anxiety as well, but despite the pouring rain Queen Alexandra drove on to the parade ground in an open carriage, to take the salute all by herself, and remain outwardly serene at the two and a half hour march-past.

When the king died in 1910 the queen was only sixty-five, but she lacked the spiritual toughness of her daughter-in-law, the new Queen Mary, and disabled by her worsening deafness she failed to make much of a new life for herself, and the remaining years became increasingly sad. However, her six grandchildren were a source of joy. When King George and Queen Mary were in India their family stayed at Sandringham, to give their grandmother a new interest in matters such as Princess May's prowess on a pony, and the elder boys' adventure at their first fox-hunt.

The traumatic years of the First World War galvanized Queen Alexandra, then aged seventy, into the kind of war-work at which

Opposite above: By 1890, this attractive trio of Princesses, Victoria Melita, Alexandra and Marie, daughters of Alfred, Duke of Edinburgh, were accomplished young riders

Below: In the same year two little Princes were enjoying one of their first debuts with a 'horse': Edward (left), who acceeded as King Edward VIII in 1936, and George, who became King George VI on his brother's abdication

she excelled, and the courage and aptitude she brought to visiting and cheering up the wounded in hospital is always associated with her name. But by the autumn of 1915, feeling worn-out and 'like a poor old cart-horse when it cannot go any further', she retreated to Sandringham. Even in that beloved home there was a new sadness when, without her comprehending at all the need for stringent national economy, it was made plain that at least some of her numerous old horses would have to be put down.

After the armistice Queen Alexandra did attend an official victory celebration in London, following down the lines of disabled ex-servicemen behind the king who was on horseback. She was in an open landau with Queen Mary, and there was an unrehearsed incident when the men broke ranks in a sudden outburst of emotion. In their efforts to shake the king's hand they almost succeeded in

In later life, King Edward VII still enjoyed riding. Seen here with a favourite pony at Sandringham

pulling him off his horse, and were only prevented from climbing into the carriage with the two queens by the escort officer who moved his horse up tight alongside. Neither of the royal ladies showed any alarm. And while the crowd of men, discipline thrown to the winds for a while, milled and jostled good-humouredly round them, Queen Alexandra sat bowing and smiling, and soothing the jangled nerves of the escort officer's horse by holding and stroking its nose in her gloved fingers.

In the remaining years, while failing health and dimming faculties took their pitiful toll, and eventually even the seemingly ageless beauty faded, the old queen was still able to enjoy a few simple pleasures, amongst them a daily visit to her stables and kennels.

Opposite above: In the early days the children of the then Duke and Duchess of York (later King George V and Queen Mary) used a Shetland pony and carriage

Below: By 1902, the two boys, Prince Albert (left) and Prince Edward (right) went riding daily with a groom, a pastime also much favoured by their sister, Princess Mary (above)

5 George V and Edward VIII
More for pleasure than prestige

Prince George, the second son of Edward VII and Queen Alexandra, who came to the throne in 1910 as King George V, began his riding career at a very early age—seated in a pannier slung from the broad back of a pony held by the queen, with his elder brother Albert Victor providing the counterpoise in a similar pannier on the other side. With such a horse-minded mother ponies inevitably played a part in Prince George's happy and boisterous childhood, and his tutor's curriculum for the early years contained riding or cricket as the alternative afternoon occupations for the brothers. But it was always intended that, as the second son, the navy should be Prince George's profession, and he became a naval cadet in 1877 when he was twelve. The next fifteen years were spent as a serving officer, until his brother's death in 1892 brought him into the immediate line of succession. And as with that other sailor, his great-grandfather William IV, riding and horses did not feature prominently in his favourite sports.

While serving with the Mediterranean Fleet in 1887 and 1888, Prince George played polo on the Marsa when ashore at Malta, in a team captained by Prince Louis of Battenberg, the Duke of Edinburgh's great-uncle. He also owned a horse there called Real Jam, which he rode out on long, enjoyable picnics. As Duke of York, and then as Prince of Wales, there were obvious ceremonial occasions to be observed on horseback. These included one in 1902, at a time when British–German relations were not at their best, and during his successful mission of goodwill to the kaiser's country the heir to the British throne rode ceremonially beside the German emperor at Potsdam. As Prince and Princess of Wales he and his wife represented the king at the wedding of Princess Ena to King Alfonso XIII of Spain—and after the ceremony their coach was only three away from that of the bride and groom, the target for a bomb which only just missed its objective. Horses and riding figured in the two visits made to India and, as king, George V made his ceremonial entry into Delhi on horseback. Unlike his father's, his big game hunting was wisely conducted from the back of an elephant!

King George always rode to take military parades and reviews, usually on his dark bay charger Brownie, but during the First World War his inspections were normally conducted on foot after arriving by car. On his second visit to the British Expeditionary Force in France, however, when the king arrived at Hesdigneul to visit the 1st Wing, Royal Flying Corps, it was suggested that the men would see him better if he were mounted, and Sir Douglas Haig loaned the king his own crowd-trained charger for the inspection. As he was about to leave this group, owing to a mis-understood order the men gave a lusty cheer at close quarters which

King George V always rode to
take military parades and
reviews, and during the First
World War he sometimes
visited his troops on a charger
Above: The King with Princess
Victoria and Sir Douglas Haig
at Aldershot in 1913. Below:
With Sir Ian Hamilton (left)
after the outbreak of war

startled his mare, and she reared, slipped on the wet ground and came down backwards, partially on her rider. The king was terribly bruised and shocked, and after a difficult, dangerous and painful journey back to England it was discovered that he had fractured his pelvis in two places.

King George had neither his father's opportunity nor his wholehearted enthusiasm for racing, but he possessed the fine racing establishment of Egerton House at Newmarket. He was not an outstandingly successful owner, but in 1925 when the royal filly Scuttle gave him his first classic, the One Thousand Guineas, King George could lay claim to being the only reigning monarch, to that date, to have both bred and owned a classic winner.

In the earlier years the king loved yacht-racing, but his favourite sport was shooting and he was an expert both with a 12-bore and with a rifle. In this connection, while riding from beat to beat at Sandringham and the adjoining estates, like Edward VII used to do, or riding on the hill at Balmoral, King George formed an affectionate and lasting partnership with a pony. This was the famous Jock, a white cob broad in the back and steady as a rock, who was a privileged member of the royal household—even known to help himself slyly from a picnic plate—who followed the king about like a dog.

Jock first became the royal shooting pony as an eight-year-old, but the king also used him for riding round the estate to visit his tenants or to inspect the home farm. A few horses, and the ponies Arabian Night and K. of K. (a Basuto pony presented by Lord Kitchener), were kept for riding in London and at Windsor, but Jock was always the favourite. As age and ill-health restricted the king's activities further, a ride on his white pony in the grounds at Sandringham became one of his chief pleasures.

When the king died in 1936 his coffin was taken from the little church at Sandringham to Wolferton station, for his last journey to London and then to Windsor. In the slow *cortège* moving along the three-mile route, to the wailing of the pipes, the new king and his brothers followed on foot behind the gun-carriage; behind the carriage carrying the queen and her daughters came Jock, led by a groom to head the procession of the king's friends and retainers.

During King George V's reign the royal 'stable' included six Daimler state limousines, a few private cars and a six-wheeled Crossley shooting-brake, in use at Sandringham and Balmoral during the last six years. When the new king, Edward VIII, went to London, to present himself to the customary Accession Privy Council on the morning after his father's death, he flew there in his own plane—to become the first British monarch ever to fly.

In the 325 days between his accession and abdication, there were occasions when the king, essentially a man of his swiftly

changing times, would have preferred to walk short distances rather than travel in the immense Daimler which was the symbol of the 'king passing by on his business'; he supplemented the traditional forms of royal transportation, the royal horses and royal cars, by creating the 'King's Flight'. By the time he was king, for relaxation he preferred to play golf, or garden, rather than ride a horse round his estates. But although he might not have minded going down in history as Edward the Innovator, he had no wish to be remembered as Edward the Reformer, and this applied also to the matter of horses.

After travelling 150,000 miles through the dominions when Prince of Wales, the king felt the necessity for getting to places in the shortest possible time. He had reason, too, for disliking traditional royal involvements with horses in other countries, where, because the animals perforce had small acquaintance with the huge and undisciplined crowds and the stresses involved, there was obvious danger to the public. On his first Canadian visit, in 1919, at the inauguration of 'Warriors Day' at the Canadian National Exhibition in Toronto, the prince was required to mount a horse for the passing down the ranks, and then riding to a platform at the side of the field. His strong preference for a car was amply justified when the veterans broke ranks, and only the sheer mass of human bodies prevented the terrified horse from bolting, as they lifted the prince off its back and passed him from hand to hand over their heads like a football. A few months later, in Melbourne, he was confronted with the traditional state landau drawn by a pair of horses, but despite his initial dismay and the tumultuous welcome nothing happened to compare with his drive through Quebec in 1927. By then the prince thought he had impressed on all the desirability of an open car for such occasions, but he had reckoned without a governor-general whose hobby was driving horses, and who brought out his liveliest pair, driven to a state landau, as a compliment to his guest. The drive commenced with a jerk that imperilled the occupants' necks; by the time they reached the suburbs the landau was lurching from side to side, with the horses very obviously bolting, and only lengthy instructions from the governor himself, delivered in French to his frantic coachman, resulted in the pair being brought at last under control.

Despite such incidents Edward had no wish to break with the pageantry of the great state occasions in Britain, and it was rain, and no desire of the king, that brought him to his first and only state opening of Parliament by car, rather than in the Irish state coach, drawn by six or four postillion horses, that is the traditional vehicle for the occasion.

King George V's family was in two distinct groups, with only three years separating the three elder children. Most of Edward's early childhood was therefore spent in the company of his brother Albert and sister Mary (in the family they were called David, Bertie and May) at York Cottage, set in the grounds of the Big House at Sandringham. As little more than toddlers the two boys were often taken for an airing in a miniature carriage, with a groom on foot, wearing a frock-coat and cockaded top-hat, in charge of the fat Shetland pony. Every Sunday afternoon when the king and queen were in residence the children were included in the York Cottage contingent, required to join their grandparents and guests for part of the progression round the grounds and gardens. This always took in the stables, where the horse-loving Queen Alexandra fed each animal with carrots; a procedure she repeated at the racing stud, while the children looked with awe at the famous Persimmon and took care to give a wide berth to the equally exalted but temperamental Diamond Jubilee. When they were old enough the boys and their sister were taught to ride, and although for a while David and Bertie gave bicycles top priority over any other means of transport, horses and ponies were an accepted part of life.

But although riding, at Balmoral or Sandringham or Windsor, was always an enjoyable part of their leave from Osborne and Dart-

The hazards of hunting appealed strongly to the Prince of Wales's adventurous spirit. Seen with Queen Maud of Norway and Queen Mary in 1920

David   Maud   Self

mouth when the two elder boys were there as naval cadets, at that time it meant more to the shy and retiring Prince Albert than to his extrovert elder brother. And it was lucky for Bertie that at Dartmouth his officer in the term realized the fact, and encouraged him in the sport which helped release the inhibitions induced by his stammer and lack of confidence in his own abilities.

With the death of his grandfather, the requirements of being heir apparent brought Edward out of the navy to university, and while there some of his winter leisure was given over to riding. At home he was much more interested in becoming a fine shot, like his father, than in cutting a fine figure on a horse. He did however consider that his riding was adequate, and was not pleased when the king disagreed and ordered Edward's equerry to improve the Prince of Wales's horsemanship. However Major Cadogan, a patient and tactful man, taught his pupil to jump with confidence, and to find

A familiar and popular figure in the shires. The Prince of Wales with hounds

enjoyment in what he had expected to be a dull chore. A day hunting with the South Oxfordshire Hounds capped this new-found interest. In 1914, a month attached to the Life Guards, with two hours each morning of mounted sword drill, riding bareback, jumping, and vaulting off and on horses at the canter, did much to further the prince's equestrian education.

During the war years, despite a commission in the Grenadier Guards and his own repeated and frustrated appeals, his 'trophy value' to the enemy kept the Prince of Wales out of the front line. His most favoured mount in France then became a bicycle—which at any rate enabled him to get acquainted at ground level with war and those who waged it. Riding on a horse was reserved for leave at Windsor.

By 1914 Prince Albert was a midshipman, but he had only just settled into the routine of the navy at war when illness kept him ashore for a while, as frustrated at being 'out of it all' as his brother. During convalescence horses helped to fill in part of the time, and he had the minor excitement of shooting a dangerous stag in the park at Windsor, which had previously attacked him and Princess Mary when out riding. In 1918, as O.C. No. 4 Squadron, Boy Wing, at what was to become the Royal Air Force Cadet College, riding, as usual, took up much of his leisure time. When he came to learn to fly, the instinctive coordination of eye and hand and brain which Prince Albert possessed as a proficient horseman and tennis player stood him in good stead.

In 1922, as Duke of York, he deputized for the king, designated 'Koom', the principal figure after the bridal couple, at the marriage of the Rumanian heir to the throne, and again good horsemanship proved an asset. The duke had the honour, and prominence, of riding immediately before the bridegroom's carriage, and his masterly and elegant control of his horse, a recent and restive import to the royal Serbian stables from Ireland, excited the full-throated acclamation of the crowds. Four months later the duke was again representing the king in the Balkans, this time for the Rumanian coronation. And again his bearing, good looks and fine horsemanship during the procession through Bucharest commanded flattering attention and made him the most popular of the royal representatives.

In 1919, as Colonel of the Welsh Guards, the Prince of Wales rode with his father at the revival of the King's Birthday Parade, a particularly splendid version of the military ceremonial duties which were to bring him out in public on horseback, until his abdication in December 1936. And it was to be in the July of that fraught year, when as King Edward VIII he was riding back from Hyde Park, at the head of the Brigade of Guards after a presentation of new colours, that a frustrated Irish journalist would hurl a loaded

Overleaf: The King with his sons (above), the Prince of Wales, the Duke of York, the Duke of Gloucester, and his son-in-law the Earl of Harewood. The King's Birthday Parade, 1928. Below left: Prince George, Duke of Kent, the King's youngest son, was also 'a good man to hounds'. Below right: Prince Albert, Duke of York, seen here in Windsor Park, 1914

revolver under his horse's feet—a shining object that could so easily have been a bomb, but which the king would totally ignore as he rode unmoved upon his way.

It was the postwar prime minister, Lloyd George, who suggested that the Prince of Wales should visit the countries of the British Commonwealth in an official capacity. And during his immensely successful tours of the many countries concerned, there were opportunities for riding in his 'off-duty' time. There was space and the necessity for horses on the 4,000-acre ranch the prince bought in Canada. During the extensive and incredible Indian tour, twenty-five polo ponies were included—along with carriage horses and landaus for the state entries into cities—on the third train of the royal entourage. At Bangalore, experienced horses were provided for the prince's initiation into the dangerous sport of pig-sticking.

At Manila, during a polo match with the U.S. Cavalry, a ball on the eyebrow necessitated three stitches. The Australian schedule allowed little time for anything, even punctuality, but in South Africa Edward sometimes relaxed on the veld, taking over a spare pony to gallop into town with the contingent of welcoming Boer farmers—incidents which not only provided needed exercise but also did a little to ease the lingering bitterness of the Boer War.

On an unconnected visit to the United States, to watch the international matches and to play polo himself, the press reports alerted the Prince of Wales to the strange American view of those days, that a polo player was synonymous with a 'playboy'. And his decision to sell his string of ponies was perhaps a wise one.

Back home, all King George's sons made a name for themselves in the hunting field, though not entirely for the same reasons. The

The Prince of Wales enjoyed many varied forms of riding. Seen here herding cattle on his Canadian ranch, 1919

For relaxation from official
duties the Prince of Wales
found the thrills and spills of
point-to-pointing as efficacious
as the excitements of the
hunting field

The King's four sons on
military duty. Left to right:
The Prince of Wales, the Duke
of York, Prince Henry and
Prince George

climate of public opinion still looked on fox-hunting as a normal
sport for those with the inclination and means, and that included
members of the royal family. What the public could not take with
the equanimity of their Victorian and Edwardian forebears were
the inevitable falls connected with the sport; misadventures which
with the future King Edward VII, also hunting as Prince of Wales,
had been regarded with some admiration as evidence of his 'pluck',
but which with the future King Edward VIII were clamorously
opposed as an unwarranted risk to the neck of the heir apparent.

The prince and his brothers were immensely popular with the
hunting fraternity of the fashionable packs they supported, in
seasons that began and often continued with the Pytchley hounds.
And riding over that formidable country was an exacting apprentice-
ship for taking on the wonderful galloping country, and well-laid
fences, of the Quorn, the Cottesmore and the Belvoir.

The Prince of Wales always felt that life must be lived to the
full. He would tackle anything in the way of a jump, and was by
nature and the very circumstances of his official life inclined to take
private risks, but it is also possible that he had no more than the
normal number of mishaps—only the maximum publicity to make
much of them. He found few thrills to equal that of riding a good
horse on a line of his own, but his hunting was combined with
the even more dangerous pastimes of point-to-point and steeplechase
riding. Both sports were calculated to prove his courage and
endurance on equal terms with others, and to take his mind off the
normal round of royal engagements.

When in India the prince, despite the protests of his staff, accepted the loan of a horse and entered for, and won, a local point-to-point—over four miles of rough country dotted with deep nullahs, ditches covered in grass, on a course that was fortunately familiar to his mount. Earlier he had won a race at the Household Brigade meeting at Hawthorn Hill, with his parents watching from the stand, to become the first heir apparent to ride in a race, let alone win it. But although the king and queen were naturally proud, they were also apprehensive about this sport, particularly when the American press became over-interested and frequently facetious, every time the Prince of Wales had a fall, however innocuous.

Unfortunately the toss he took in 1924, when he fell at the first fence in the army point-to-point at Arborfield Cross, resulted in concussion, entailing a month in bed, the first week in a darkened room. The public outcry flared up once more, a question was asked in the House, and the prince was begged by the prime minister and by the king not to expose himself further to the dangers of race-riding. In fact it was not until after King George's illness at the end of 1928 that the prince agreed to give up racing, at the request of his mother. And since his hunters were all potential 'chasers' he sold them also.

The difference in character between the Prince of Wales and the Duke of York was borne out in their approach to riding. Both were full of courage, but where the elder brother's horsemanship was abounding in spectacular dash, so that he participated in a number of high-powered equestrian sports in a relatively short while, the younger was interested, as always, in assimilating all the fundamentals. In less of a hurry than the Prince of Wales, the duke turned himself into the best horseman of his family. He proved an admirable rider to hounds and hunting was a favourite sport until, partly of necessity, his father's shooting interests gained him as a brilliant convert. But in the winter of 1923–4, the duke and duchess took a house conveniently placed for the Pytchley and Whaddon Chase, and from here the duke hunted as often as his engagements allowed.

His liking for the sport continued, and it was a sad decision to sell his horses and give up hunting, following the royal line of strict economy in the financial crisis in May 1931, but until ill-health precluded it the love of riding never waned.

The traumatic years of the Second World War allowed little time or thought for horses, but after his accession King George VI still liked to ride before breakfast whenever he could. The country and country life were his delight, and he and the queen brought up their young daughters to share the same interests. As soon as they were old enough, one of the king's greatest pleasures was to go riding in Windsor Park with Elizabeth and Margaret on their ponies.

6 The Royal Family Today
Royal horses are still important

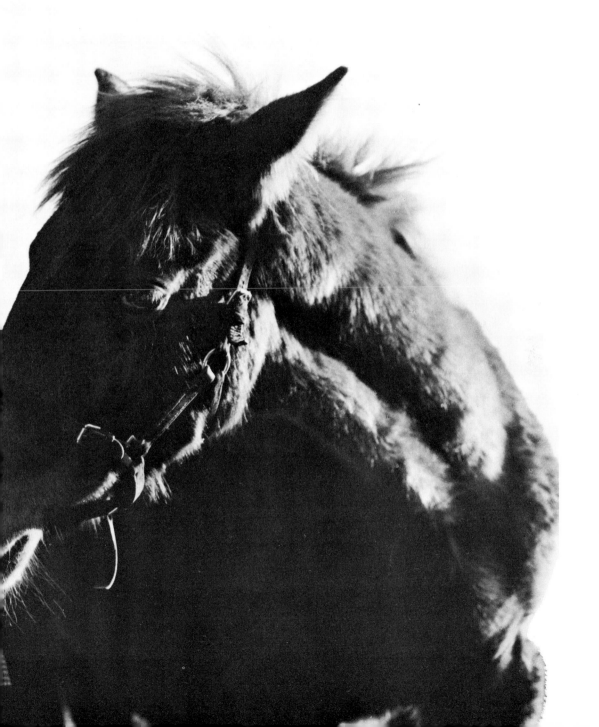

Previous pages: The Queen's
feeling for horses extends to all
types. Seen here at
Sandringham with the foal
Oporto, sired by a stallion
presented to her by the
President of Portugal. At first,
Oporto was one of the Queen's
own riding horses; sub-
sequently he became an Event
horse

The last lingering role of horses as part of everyday British life had vanished some while before the Second World War, and there were even those to predict that in the speeded-up technological age to come, future generations would only be able to get acquainted with horses and ponies in zoos. In the jet age it might also seem logical to have thought that the ancient link between the monarchy and horses would have receded into the past.

Yet after the war people started to rediscover the rewarding partnership possible with a horse or pony. Now, while scientists prepare to rocket far beyond the moon, more and more people each year are finding personal adventure in riding, and a satisfying and living dimension to an existence largely mechanized. As part of this climate of thought, and although obviously changed in character, the connection between horses and the throne has remained strong.

Nowadays the only time the state horses and carriages take on the 'station work' normal in the Victorian era, and still usual practice when King George V was on the throne, is when some head of state arrives on an official visit. Nowadays the royal family travel the thousands of miles included in their annual schedules by plane and helicopter and car. But fortunately only a minority look on the splendid royal equipages that appear on ceremonial occasions as anachronisms, and there are few to maintain that a gleaming motorcade would still fit the bill, even if it might be less disruptive to the urgent life of the London streets. Equally fortunately the queen and her advisers, while fully aware that with changed times and altered opinions the monarchy must, to some extent, change too, also appreciate the importance of preserving the 'touch of magic' that surrounds the throne.

And so, when the queen goes in state to open parliament she still drives in splendour in the Irish state coach, drawn by the Windsor Greys decked out in one of the magnificent sets of red morocco state harness, and controlled by postillions resplendent in liveries of scarlet and gold. Weather permitting, the attractions of Royal Ascot are still immensely enhanced by the royal procession driving down the course in open Ascot landaus. Royal brides are still conveyed to and from Westminster Abbey in the fairy-tale glass coach, purchased for King George V's coronation in 1911. Ambassadors are driven to the Palace to present their credentials to the queen in either a state landau or in King Edward VII's town coach, and twice a day the royal mail, which goes 'by hand', is collected and delivered at Buckingham Palace by a one-horse brougham. On all the great ceremonial occasions, history and tradition are still brought to life, and colour and beauty offered to the eye, whether the beholder is there in the flesh to line the streets or sitting at home looking at television. The tourist trade too is

boosted by the presence of horses and carriages, harness and liveries, which are all part of the national inheritance.

Apart from the state animals, the other royal horses and ponies might be thought to be little more than a pleasant adjunct to the royal family's leisure. Unlike her great-great-grandmother, the queen and her household if in need of exercise can scarcely set out in a 'cavalcade' to ride the surrounding streets—modern traffic and press coverage forbid it. Nor does the queen, in the manner of the youthful Queen Victoria, discuss affairs of the nation with her prime minister whilst cantering side by side in the Park—she confers with him once a week in the strict seclusion of the Palace. But the pressures of modern royal life; the very speed and mileage involved in its numerous and extensive commitments; the technical marvels of television and satellite that bring the royal family under the clearest, closest scrutiny by millions of people all over the world; the increasing curiosity of the public to know more and more about the home life of today's public figures; all these add up to stresses and strains unimaginable to royalty of past eras. An absorbing pastime, where the participant has the opportunity to be 'out on his own', is an essential ingredient of modern royal life. And since this is an outlet that horses can provide for many members of the family, in particular for the queen, Prince Philip and Princess

As children Princess Elizabeth and Princess Margaret loved ponies

Overleaf: It was natural that Princess Elizabeth should wish her fourteenth birthday portrait (left) to include a favourite grey pony – the same grey of Welsh breeding that Princess Margaret (right) also loved to ride

Anne, they still fulfil a most necessary and important function.

As a child the queen, then Princess Elizabeth, was as 'pony mad' as most other young girls lucky enough to have the opportunity of riding. Her parents, then the Duke and Duchess of York, were anxious that both she and her sister, Princess Margaret, should have as 'normal' a childhood as possible, but even before the duke became king, and Elizabeth heir presumptive, it was impossible for their lives to be really free of the limits imposed by their position. Afterwards, this aspect was emphasized, the publicity angle increased even more, and ponies played an important part in a life that included few 'unofficial' excursions into the outside world.

The duchess rode enthusiastically as a girl, so that she as well as the duke fostered the children's love of riding, and the countrified life where ponies and dogs held a cherished position.

By today's standards, and compared with the freedom that Princess Anne has been able to enjoy, it was perhaps a very limited existence, although a very happy one And the fact that from the age of thirteen Princess Elizabeth grew up in a world at war, where there was little or no social life for anyone, made her and her sister even more dependent on their own resources. At the outbreak of war the royal family were at Balmoral, and the princesses stayed on in Scotland for some months. They continued their lessons, but were able to spend their free time in the company of the couple of ponies which, with only a little help from the skeleton wartime staff, they themselves thoroughly enjoyed looking after. Riding, driving and teaching the ponies tricks, 'out on their own' to a degree never experienced before, proved a delight, and this was the kind of life they continued when the royal lodge at Windsor became their permanent home until the end of hostilities.

As the princesses grew up, horses replaced the ponies for riding, but there was a lot of excitement at the 1943 Royal Windsor Horse Show, when Elizabeth, then seventeen, drove a Fell pony to take a first prize, and then won a Driving Class the next year with her sister's pony, Hans.

The queen has never emulated her great-great-grandmother by taking a military review, as such, on horseback, but at the age of twenty-one, mounted side-saddle on a mannered ex-hunter especially trained for the occasion and riding in the traditional position of heir to the throne, she accompanied the king at the Trooping the Colour, the ceremony for the Sovereign's Official Birthday Parade. Like Queen Victoria she was wearing a special dark blue 'uniform', and her appearance on horseback created the same delighted response from the public.

The next year the king was not well enough to ride, and the princess rode beside his carriage, after that deputizing for her father

Pages 118–19: King George VI liked nothing better than to ride in the royal parks, and the company of his daughters added to the enjoyment

Previous pages: Princess Elizabeth first rode at the Sovereign's Official Birthday Parade in 1947 (left) when, wearing a dark blue uniform and riding an ex-hunter, she accompanied her father on Horseguards Parade. Soon illness prevented the King from riding, and the Princess deputized for him. Since becoming Queen she has, with few exceptions, taken the salute each year at this spectacular military ceremony (right)

Opposite: The Queen has always taught her children when young how to 'tack up' their own ponies and given them their first 'feel of a pony'. Seen here in 1964 out in the grounds of Balmoral with Prince Andrew on his Shetland, Valkyrie, and his cousin David, Lord Linley

until his death. Since she came to the throne, with few exceptions the queen has taken the salute at this annual and spectacular military ceremony.

Wearing the becoming, adapted uniform of a colonel-in-chief of the Foot Guards, mounted on a handsome police horse chosen for its impeccable ceremonial behaviour as well as charger-like appearance, escorted by the Duke of Edinburgh, the Duke of Kent and other high-ranking officers and officials, the queen rides up the Mall to Horse Guards Parade, where her natural dignity sets the tone for the ensuing splendid spectacle, before she returns to the Palace at the head of the Queen's Guard.

This is the only time the queen rides side-saddle and, always meticulous, she puts in some weeks of practice beforehand. It is also the only time the queen appears in public on horseback, unless one counts the strictly unofficial royal scamper up the course during Ascot week—inaugurated by the queen as a girl, confined to the royal family and their guests, and nowadays always won by Princess Anne—at which neither press nor public are encouraged.

In private the queen rides whenever she can and that means, apart from the holidays at Sandringham and Balmoral, most week-ends at Windsor. She has a great affinity with her horses and loves riding as a sport; for her it is the perfect relaxation in a very exacting life. The crown equerry or the stud groom usually accompanies the queen when she rides in the parks at Windsor, but in the greater privacy of the Sandringham or Balmoral estates she may take out a horse by herself, to enjoy an hour or so of the seclusion that is essential to one of her nature.

The queen may not be quite such a speed merchant as her daughter, but she loves a good gallop with Princess Anne over the open Norfolk fields, or cantering along the wide rides cut through the surrounding Sandringham woods. In Scotland Anne seldom rides on the hills, where the tortuous stony tracks, winding through heather and past peat bog, make the pace too slow for her taste, but here the queen often has the company of Princess Margaret, still also a keen horsewoman, and of her competent children with their ponies—even if David Linley's liking for speed is in tune with his cousin Anne's. Sometimes the queen's younger sons, Andrew and Edward, may join the party, although in recent years other pursuits have largely taken over from riding. When they were younger the queen enjoyed teaching them the first stages, how to saddle and bridle and generally cope with their Shetland pony, just as she once taught Charles and Anne. But although she used to take them out round the estates on foot, and later occasionally on a leading rein, neither Andrew nor Edward showed quite the same interest as their elder brother and sister. Nor did the queen enjoy

Horses provide the royal
family with most necessary
relaxation. Left: The Queen
and Princess Margaret
returning from a mounted
inspection of the cross-country
course at Badminton Three-
Day Horse Trials in 1959.
Twelve years later the Queen
and Prince Philip were finding
horses the best and most
enjoyable means of watching
the coaching marathon in
Windsor Great Park (below)

a repetition of the fun during the Easter holidays at Windsor, in the years when she used to drive her car in pursuit of Anne, or Charles, batting round the Park over a miniature cross-country, or galloping through the ancient trees laying a trail for a mounted paper-chase.

The queen's riding horses are housed in the Royal Mews at Windsor, with one or two taken to Sandringham or Balmoral for holiday riding. Through the years many of them have arrived as gifts, like the Arab from King Hussein of Jordan way back in 1958, the Thoroughbred from the President of Pakistan in 1959, and a Lusitano stallion from the President of Portugal. There is the Canadian-bred mare, presented by the 'Mounties', and now combining the duties of royal charger for the Trooping the Colour with those of favourite hack, and another from the same source arrived as stable mate in 1973. And then there was the other beloved black mare, of more character than breeding, which was given by a local farmer and remained 'top of the stables' for years. Others have included a would-be steeplechaser, bred by the late king, which declined to 'chase', several bred as polo ponies which either grew too big or were eschewed by Prince Philip, and at least one of the queen's well-loved race-horses whose legs had become 'suspect' for the course. Royal Ocean, one of Princess Anne's first eventers, is

ending his days as a riding horse at Windsor.

Although the late king was not a racing enthusiast, he always took a keen interest in the royal racing studs and was delighted to get the occasional winner. His wife, Queen Elizabeth, began her successful ownership of steeplechasers with Monaveen, a horse she shared with her daughter, then Princess Elizabeth. As queen-mother she has owned some great horses like The Rip and Laffy, and the luckless Devon Loch which all but won the National, and is a frequent and loved visitor to the courses where her animals run. By December 1972 she had notched up her 250th steeplechase winner.

Like Queen Victoria's Thoroughbreds, the queen's are bred at Hampton Court, and at the nearby Polhampton stud which is leased. Racing is a sport that the queen finds really absorbing in all its aspects. She loves to attend as many of the classics as time will permit—which is not a great number in the year—but her special interest lies in the fact that many of the horses she watches in person, or on television, competing on the course have been bred according to her own ideas. She owns the great stallion Aureole, which was bred by the late king, has a part-share in Ribero, which is now the principal sire at Sandringham, and always works out the mating programmes for her own stud mares. As one who takes time and trouble really to know her subject, whatever it may be, the queen

The wide open expanse of stubble fields at Sandringham provide good riding country – and galloping ground – for the Queen and Princess Anne

Above and opposite: Prince Philip took up polo after the war, and his natural ability combined with expert tuition from Lord Louis Mountbatten to make him a first-class player. He found the speed and toughness of the game exactly suited to his will to win and his need of violent exercise

has made such an intensive study of the intricate Thoroughbred blood lines, that she is now one of the few acknowledged world experts.

But Thoroughbreds are not the only horses the queen is interested in breeding. Some of the riding horses, and one or two of the children's ex-ponies have been loaned to suitable studs, including Valkyrie, the engaging Shetland mare that was a present to the queen from the people of the Shetland Isles in 1960, and with which Prince Andrew established what his mother termed 'an association'. At Balmoral most of the Highland and Fell deer and shooting ponies are home-bred, and through the years one or two of the Cleveland Bay carriage horses in the mews at Buckingham Palace have been bred at the queen's instigation at Sandringham. That is also where some of Prince Philip's best and favourite ex-polo ponies are ending their days as brood mares, and for years it was one of the queen's ambitions to breed suitable animals for her husband to play. Unfortunately she had little luck in this side of her hobby, as either the ponies grew too big for the game, or Prince Philip failed to get on with them.

Prince Philip rode a little as a boy, and before his commitments grew quite so extensive he enjoyed a certain amount of 'family riding' when his elder children were young. But the polo that he started after the war under the expert tuition of Earl Mountbatten of Burma, then Lord Louis Mountbatten, proved exactly the tough, fast game best suited to his competitive spirit and need for violent exercise, and soon took up any time Prince Philip had to spare. With his usual two hundred per cent involvement in the matter in hand, he set about turning himself into a top-notch player, well known for the speed of his ponies and the strength and determination of his attack. He captained the Windsor team for many seasons, and survived a number of crashing falls which included a few injuries. The prince's polo season was of necessity short, but he crammed as much play into it as he could, and any spare half-hour was devoted to practice—usually on the lawn adjoining Windsor Castle, to the detriment of the grass.

Prince Philip had always said he would give up polo when he was fifty, and recurring wrist trouble strengthened his resolve, but it must have been a bad moment when he jumped off his pony after the last chukka, in the last game of his final season of 1971. Fortunately there was a new sport to hand.

Two or three years previously the Polish delegate to the Fédération Equestre Internationale (the F.E.I.), of which Prince Philip is president, had suggested that some international rules ought to be drawn up for a driving competition. In common with most people in Britain, the prince knew little or nothing of com-

petitive driving, a sport which was then almost exclusively European, but as the result of his interest a competition was devised, based on the riding Three-Day Event, and Prince Philip himself started to learn to drive.

He began with a single horse, progressed to a pair and, by then fascinated, set out to achieve the very difficult art of driving a four-in-hand. As usual there were no holds barred; most of his spare moments now go into driving practice on the miniature obstacle 'courses' laid out at Windsor and Sandringham for the purpose; by 1973 he had become an international competitor.

Keen as he is, Prince Philip does not aspire to the heights of someone like Auguste Dubay, the current world champion from Switzerland, who has been competing for around twenty years and reckons to drive for six hours each day. But he has found an absorbing sport with which he reckons to be able to cope for another ten or fifteen years before having to look for something else. And although there are few if any contestants under fifty, and the majority are considerably older, this is no game of tiddly-winks, but calls for both skill and good nerve. The marathon course for Phase B, the cross-country section of the European Driving Championship held in Windsor Great Park in 1973, provided a sufficiency of thrills and spills to prove the point, as Prince Philip was to discover for himself.

He was driving a team of part-bred Cleveland Bays to a Balmoral dog cart exhibited by the queen, the horses more normally employed in trotting decorously along the London streets with one or another of the royal equipages, or adding glamour to the procession for some ceremonial state occasion.

The prince had first to cope with the two divisions of Phase A —Presentation, in which the condition of the vehicle, the horses and harness is taken into account, and marks added or subtracted for the sufficiency of the spares carried (extra traces, reins, etc.), the correct dress of the Whip, including his driving gloves, and that of the grooms, and the suitability of the horses' shoes. For the second division, the Dressage, Prince Philip had to perform various movements similar to those required in ridden Dressage—extended trot, collected trot, working trot, walking, reining back—which are far from simple to perform with four animals which may or may not be of a single mind.

The second day of the contest found Prince Philip going off in his turn in the wake of teams varying in type from Welsh Cobs to German Holsteins, from chestnut Wielkopolskas from Poland and Hungarian Kisberers, to Irish Greys or picturesque medieval black Friesians from Holland, the vehicles a miscellany with romantic names such as Beaufort phaeton or eszterhazy or good plain brake.

In this phase the competitors cover many miles, and the five

Opposite: In 1971, Prince Philip gave up polo, but quickly found another sport to suit his tastes – competitive driving, where manoeuvering a four-in-hand around a cross-country course can provide enough excitement, and hazard, for anyone!

sections are timed—two of them precisely—and have to be done as ordained at walk or trot. And this was where Prince Philip might have slipped back in time a century or two, as he drove through dappled sunshine under great trees that have shadowed many royal excursions and equipages, and a few royal Whips as well. The air was free of the stench and pollution of petrol fumes, and though the jets from Heathrow still thundered overhead they could be ignored in the rhythmic beat of many sets of iron-shod hooves, punctuated by the tinkling harness bells of the Hungarians, the blood-stirring notes of a coaching horn or two and, since the voice is an acknowledged aid in driving, by encouraging cries or angry admonitions in a variety of different languages.

The horses splashed merrily through the eighty-yard wide water splash—or stood teetering anxiously on the edge; there were sharp turns up banks and through trees to negotiate, and artificial obstacles where the minimum of space called for pin-point driving at the walk. Visually it was beautiful, to attempt it was a satisfying test, to perform it proved excitingly hazardous.

The crown equerry was one of those to turn his vehicle over, and Prince Philip came to grief at the pit-props, not entirely to his surprise since he knew his leaders' aversion to piles of logs. But when they jinked and their driver took action to straighten them out, the wheelers then came across a little, just caught the wheel hub on a log, and that was that. One might drag home with a broken back axle, but with the front one gone and the wheel pulled out the dog cart was completely 'boss-eyed'.

Calamities or no, by 8.30 the next morning Prince Philip was walking the course for Phase 3, obstacle-driving with a tight time limit in the confined space of a show-ring, similar to the Eventer's show-jumping phase, and calling for expert control and precision.

Each hazard consists of two cone-shaped plastic markers, with a ball on top which topples at the slightest touch, and with just room enough for the wheels to pass between. They are set at angles demanding acute turns, and figures of eight, with sometimes a stretch to be driven in and out like a bending race, and 'doubles' where failure at the second element means starting again at the first. To be successful, instant obedience, from horses tuned to a peak of physical fitness for the cross-country driving, is a difficult but essential 'must'. Prince Philip brought his team in to limber up at a nice steady pace before being given the 'off'. Then it was 'Trot on! Trot on!' as he swung his horses skilfully round the course, to conclude with a sharp and obviously enjoyable canter up the straight, leaning forward to urge them: 'Come on! Come on! Come on!' as he passed the finishing line within time and without penalty.

After Prince Philip gave up polo for driving, there was still Prince Charles to carry the flag on the polo field, and give the queen further enjoyable Sunday afternoons watching games on Smith's Lawn in the Park. As a serving naval officer he now has little time, except for the odd game when on leave and the occasional chance to sample the polo grounds in Malta or other countries where his ship puts in. But before he joined the navy the prince was as enthusiastic about polo as his father, and although not yet quite in the same class as Prince Philip's above-average handicap rating of five goals, he shows much promise. When the 1972 match between England and America for the historic Coronation Cup was staged at Cowdray, a second game, Young England versus Young America, was included, and Prince Charles proved his worth. He captained the team, and his goal in the third chukka put England ahead although, after dead-heating, the requisite 'sudden death' chukka then gave Young America the match. The prince's forceful play and tactical soundness rated him far above his handicap.

As a boy, Prince Charles found a lot of enjoyment with ponies, but polo, begun with his father's encouragement in 1964, proved to be his sport. Seen here at Windsor in the early days, practising with the co-operation of Prince Philip's ex-polo pony, San Quanina

Opposite: Princess Anne combines her mother's 'rapport' with a horse, with her father's determination to go in and win . . . if possible. In 1971, the Princess and Doublet, bred by the Queen, became European Three-Day Event Champion, and the Princess was voted Sportswoman of the Year.

With the help of Alison Oliver, the Princess schools her own horses and puts in a lot of hard work. She loves the freedom that her chosen sport, Eventing, brings her; she can take bad luck and failure as well as success. Below: Columbus and Princess Anne at the Windsor Horse Trials, 1972. All this stems from those years when Princess Anne discovered the joy of going across country on her beloved Irish pony, High Jinks (right)

Until he went to boarding school, and new interests and hobbies took over, a period which coincided with out-growing a particularly loved pony, Prince Charles much enjoyed riding, and did a certain amount of competing at Pony Club level—although with never quite the same single-hearted purpose as his sister. And it was perhaps the realization that Anne was always just that much better than he was—and was never backward in giving advice—that was another factor in later keeping Charles off horseback almost completely until he was about sixteen. Then his father's gift of an old polo pony aroused a feeling for the game and the animals that go with it, which was to grow into an absorbing pastime.

Horses and ponies play a part in the leisure activities of most of the other branches of the royal family. The Duke of Kent has found enjoyment in the hunting field, and both he and the duchess have always ridden when the opportunity offered. Their daughter Marina is very keen, and a dedicated pony fan, and while living in London both she and her brother James were able to ride in Richmond Park. Now that the family have their country home in the horse-minded county of Norfolk, no doubt riding will become an increasingly popular recreation with them all.

As a child, and before marriage, the duke's sister, Princess Alexandra, rated riding as one of her top pleasures, and she is a very good horsewoman. Both she and her husband, Mr Ogilvie, still enjoy the sport, and are bringing up their children with the same interests, but their many pressing activities nowadays allow little time for it themselves.

There are other members of the family who play polo or ride for pleasure, but of them all Princess Anne is the one whose riding activities and love of horses have brought her world prominence. And maybe she has always had most need of what horses and ponies can offer the royal family today.

When she was quite a tiny child Anne became involved, as a matter of course, in her mother's horse and pony interests, but she needed little encouragement. At seven she was fully capable of controlling her lively little pony William, riding 'solo' on family excursions in the Park, and the Mews at Windsor remained a favourite haunt until she left school. Anne has inherited the queen's instinctive 'way with a horse', and as a child was always confident that she could cope with any animal, however unsuitable, on which she would optimistically try to cajole a ride. She began competing in Pony Club Hunter Trials and their like while she was still quite young, and to this she brought the same will to win displayed by her father, tempered by a sympathetic *rapprochement* with her pony.

Princess Anne set a precedent for a daughter of the British sovereign when she went to boarding school, and there she tasted a freedom that went way beyond the comparative, and again unprecedented, liberty she had already enjoyed through ponies and competing. Her good pony High Jinks went to school too, staying at a nearby excellent riding establishment where Anne went for a weekly lesson with him; and where it quickly became apparent that both he and his rider had a long way to go in acquiring the unpopular disciplines of dressage!

It was here that her instructor's enthusiasm first inspired Anne to consider Eventing as her own particular branch of equestrian competing. It is an occupation which remains on an 'amateur' footing, and which combines the riding qualities and high standards of horse training demanded by Dressage, with all the excitement and courage of riding across country—as well as the versatility of a horse and rider able to show-jump.

Even in those early days there were none of the short cuts to success that money can sometimes buy. None of Anne's ponies had ever been wonderfully bred, expensive animals, ready-made winners in some particular field. When she acquired her loved Jinks, he was a well-made, willing young all-rounder, but as inexperienced as his rider. And in the field of junior Eventing, where they began to make their mark, Anne and her pony had to learn the job from the bottom. When she took on Purple Star, her first horse, he was and has remained a delightful character but was a complete novice. Her famous Doublet was bred by the queen as a potential polo pony, and when he grew too big and eventually went to Alison Oliver, the princess's trainer, as a 'possible' for the princess to Event, he was temperamentally far from easy and his potential was quite unknown. And although Goodwill, acquired in the autumn of 1972 and soon upgraded to top Eventing, was a Grade A show-jumper when bought, he knew nothing whatever about this very different sport.

It would never occur to Anne to do it any other way, and for her the satisfaction of success comes principally from the fact that, with the expert help of Alison Oliver, and a great deal of strenuous hard work on her own part, she achieves it herself.

Apart from other considerations, the very speed with which Princess Anne made the international scene in what is acknowledged as one of the toughest of sports, is a remarkable achievement. She came into adult Eventing after leaving school in July 1968, when she was seventeen. She and Jinks had been doing very well in the junior competitions, but this was something very different.

It was not an easy time for the princess, anyway. After four years of being, in term-time, just 'one of the crowd', and at the moment when her school friends were all embarking on jobs and flats of their own, a return to the inevitable restrictions of royal life seemed a difficult task. Only with horses could Anne find, after a

while, a world where she was accepted solely on merit. If she could ride, she could ride, but it had nothing whatever to do with who she was, and she set out to prove the point.

There were additional problems not encountered by other competitors, and one of these was time. The princess was embarking on her first rounds of public duties and although, since she considers them part of 'the job', she would never think of evading them, it does often mean that while her rivals continue with their uninterrupted training programmes, Princess Anne is flying off somewhere, sometimes for a week or more. And although to the uninitiated it might seem perfectly feasible for Alison Oliver to take on all the schooling, and produce a perfectly trained horse on to which the princess has only to climb and 'press the right buttons', horses and competing just do not work that way—success comes with the partnership and confidence that gradually builds up between rider and horse. Another trouble was the understandable but over-enthusiastic attentions of the press and spectators, somewhat nerve-racking to the rider and sometimes dangerously distracting to the horse.

One-Day Horse Trials are one thing, and Three-Day Events another. Some of the basics are similar but the Event calls for a different class of riding, endurance and courage, and often for a different type of horse. Success in the easier trials enabled Anne to qualify Doublet for Badminton in 1971, next to the Olympics and European Championship the toughest competition in the Eventing world. Speculation was rife. Would the queen and Prince Philip let her compete? *Should* she compete, when both she and her horse were so relatively inexperienced? Would she even get round?

Princess Anne and Doublet did get round, fifth out of forty-eight, and would have been fourth but for the nervous tension which gave them a fault in the show-jumping phase. The winner was Lt Mark Phillips with his horse Great Ovation.

After more and mounting speculation and some weeks of tension, Princess Anne was asked to ride as an individual in the European Championships at Burghley in that same autumn. Her hopes seemed dashed when she had to go into hospital for a serious operation only six weeks beforehand, but she got herself fit with the aid of a crash get-fit course, worked out while still in bed, and a great deal of grit and determination.

And she and Doublet won, to become the Individual European Champions, and well in the running for inclusion in the British Olympic Three-Day Event team, going to Munich in the next year.

Princess Anne did go to Munich, but because Doublet had injured a tendon she went as a spectator and saw the British team, which included Mark Phillips, win the gold medal.

Opposite: Riding, Eventing and the horse she loves provide the Princess with the freedom and independence she needs. They also provide her with a world where she is accepted 'on a level', and judged on her ability alone

On Tuesday, 29 May 1973, Princess Anne and Lt Mark Phillips announced the happy news of their engagement, and they are to be married on 14 November of the same year. Horses were the common link that first brought about their meeting, and amongst the many and varied views and interests that they will share in the future, horses will again rank high.

A pony was one of Mark Phillips's first real presents, and as a schoolboy he rode in the Beaufort Hunt Pony Club horse trials team for five successive years, getting to the finals on three occasions. His first big competition was in 1967 when he rode Rock On at Burghley to come fourth, and the same position at Badminton the next year against stiff opposition earned him the position of reserve rider for the Olympic Games in Mexico.

In 1969 he competed as an individual in the European Championships at Haras du Pin, and riding the loaned Chicago helped the British team win the world championships a year later at Punchestown.

Mark and Great Ovation won Badminton in 1972 as well as in 1971, but despite their great record together the horse was disappointing at Munich, and a disastrous cross-country rather offset their good Dressage marks and brilliant clear in the show-jumping phase.

All this time Princess Anne and Lt Phillips had been meeting as friends and rivals in the Eventing competitions. They had genuine admiration for each other's horsemanship and achievements, which were an endless source of mutually interesting conversation. When Princess Anne failed to hold her Columbus on the steeplechase course at Burghley in 1972, she lent the powerful young horse, which had always been a handful, to Mark, and in turn they both rode, and fell off, each other's animals. At Badminton in 1973 the princess had a good round with Goodwill to come eighth, but Columbus gave the lieutenant a somewhat rough ride, with a crashing fall at one of the Luckington Lane fences and an uncalled-for ducking later on in the lake.

Soon the rumours of a royal romance were gaining strength, and before long the attentions of the press photographers were getting beyond accepted limits. It was obvious that such an expected event as an engagement must be top-line news, but apart from the personal and very private feelings of the two most concerned at such a time, there was the added problem of trying to school their very spirited and sensitive horses while the environs of Alison Oliver's stables appeared to be swarming with strangers.

It is not easy for those not horse-minded to appreciate that upsetting the training of a couple of horses could really matter to their owners, but Princess Anne and her future husband, now

Captain Phillips, take their competing seriously. At the time there was the strong hope that Princess Anne would be able to defend her title with Doublet at the European Championships to be held in Kiev, and in the future they intend to continue with the competitive riding which means so much to both of them.

These two have of course a great deal in common which has nothing to do with horses, but it was the opportunity that horses gave Princess Anne to be 'out on her own' that brought about the crossing of their paths. In the past horses have been one of the monarchy's sources of fighting power and prestige; today they offer an outlet from modern pressures and stresses. Now horses have unwittingly helped to bring happiness and marriage to the queen's only daughter.

Princess Anne and Captain Mark Phillips met through the sport they both enjoy, and in the years to come horses will continue to be one of their shared interests

Photo acknowledgments

Camera Press Ltd: 128
Fores Ltd, London: 32-3
Fox Photos Ltd: 125 (inset), 138
Godfrey Argent Ltd: 6-7, 70-1, 112-13,
123, 126-7, 133, 135 (top right)
Tim Graham: 76, 77
Keystone Press Agency Ltd: 118-19,
124-5 (top), 129, 134
Lutterworth Press: 65, 67, 78
Mansell Collection: 15, 16 (top right)
Mary Evans Picture Library: 38-9
(bottom)
National Portrait Gallery: 28 (inset)
Overseas Photo & Feature Agency
Ltd: 66, 68, 69, 72, 73, 79
Radio Times Hulton Picture Library:
8, 13, 16 (bottom), 18, 22-3, 28-9, 34,
36, 38-9 (top), 40, 44-5, 47, 48, 50, 85
(top), 88-9, 92-3
Reproduced by gracious permission of
Her Majesty the Queen: 2, 3, 52-3, 54-5,
56, 58-9, 60, 61, 62, 63, 82, 83, 84, 86,
90, 91, 95, 96-7, 99, 101, 102, 104-5,
106-7, 108-9, 110, 115, 116-17, 120, 121
Syndication International: 74, 75, 80,
130, 135 (bottom), 141